THE COMPLETE BOOK OF ENOCH

STANDARD ENGLISH VERSION

DR. JAY WINTER

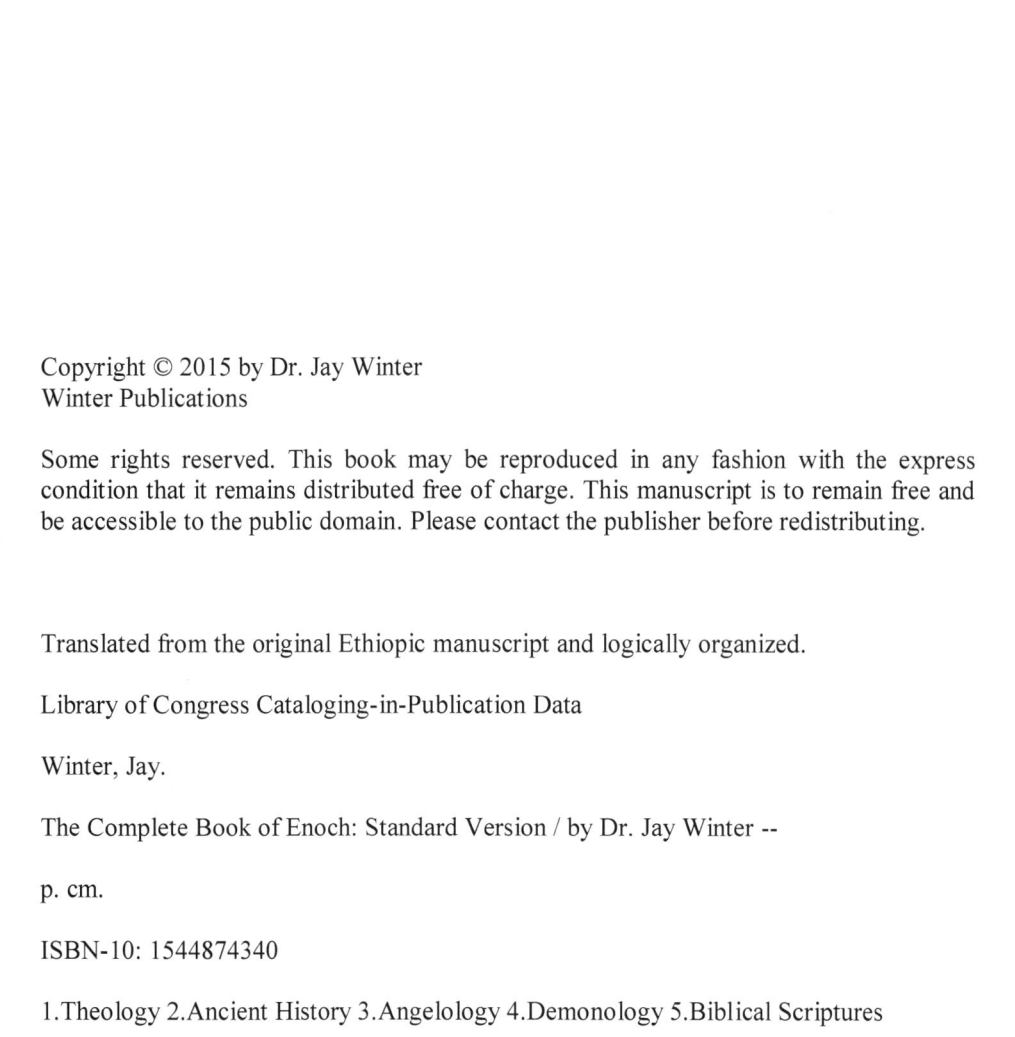

Copyright © 2015 by Dr. Jay Winter
Winter Publications

Some rights reserved. This book may be reproduced in any fashion with the express condition that it remains distributed free of charge. This manuscript is to remain free and be accessible to the public domain. Please contact the publisher before redistributing.

Translated from the original Ethiopic manuscript and logically organized.

Library of Congress Cataloging-in-Publication Data

Winter, Jay.

The Complete Book of Enoch: Standard Version / by Dr. Jay Winter --

p. cm.

ISBN-10: 1544874340

1.Theology 2.Ancient History 3.Angelology 4.Demonology 5.Biblical Scriptures

TABLE OF CONTENTS

Introduction - About the Book of Enoch	001
Book 1 - Watchers - Ch. 1 - Blessing of Enoch	008
Book 1 - Watchers - Ch. 2 - The Creation	009
Book 1 - Watchers - Ch. 3 - The Fallen Angels	011
Book 1 - Watchers - Ch. 4 - Intercession of Angels	013
Book 1 - Watchers - Ch. 5 - Book of the Words of Righteousness	017
Book 1 - Watchers - Ch. 6 - Taken by Angels	021
Book 1 - Watchers - Ch. 7 - The Holy Angels	023
Book 2 - Parables - Ch. 1 - The First Parable	032
Book 2 - Parables - Ch. 2 - The Second Parable	037
Book 2 - Parables - Ch. 3 - The Third Parable	045
Book 3 - Book of Noah - Ch. 1 - Birth of Noah	054
Book 3 - Book of Noah - Ch. 2 - Calling Enoch	057
Book 3 - Book of Noah - Ch. 3 - Judgment of Angels	059
Book 3 - Book of Noah - Ch. 4 - Secrets of the Parables	061
Book 4 - Kingdom of Heaven - Ch. 1 - Enoch is Taken	066
Book 4 - Kingdom of Heaven - Ch. 2 - The Luminaries of Heaven	069
Book 4 - Kingdom of Heaven - Ch. 3 - Heavenly Tablets	079
Book 4 - Kingdom of Heaven - Ch. 4 - One Year to Record	081
Book 4 - Kingdom of Heaven - Ch. 5 - Visions	085
Book 5 - Epistle of Enoch - Ch. 1 - Guidance of Enoch	100
Book 5 - Epistle of Enoch - Ch. 2 - Wisdom of Enoch	103
Book 5 - Epistle of Enoch - Ch. 3 - Wisdom of Enoch	109
Book 5 - Epistle of Enoch - Ch. 4 - Wisdom of Enoch	115
Book 5 - Epistle of Enoch - Ch. 5 - Wisdom of Enoch	117
Book 5 - Epistle of Enoch - Ch. 6 - Revelation of Enoch	119

EXTRAS

Book of the Giants	123
Evidence of Giants	137
References to Enoch in Other Manuscripts	147
Testament of Solomon	153

About the Book of Enoch

(Also known as "Ethiopian Enoch")

The Book of Enoch (also known as 1 Enoch) was once cherished by Jews and Christians alike, this book later fell into disfavor with powerful theologians - precisely because of its controversial statements on the nature and deeds of the fallen angels.

The Enochian writings, in addition to many other writings that were excluded (or lost) from the Bible (i.e., the Book of Tobit, Esdras, etc.) were widely recognized by many of the early church fathers as "Apocryphal" writings. The term "apocrypha" is derived from the Greek word meaning "hidden" or "secret". Originally, the import of the term may have been complimentary in that the term was applied to sacred books whose contents were too exalted to be made available to the general public.

In Dan. 12:9-10 we hear of words that are shut up until the end of time and, words that the wise shall understand and the wicked shall not. In addition, 4 Ezra 14:44ff. mentions 94 books, of which 24 (the OT) were to be published and 70 were to be delivered only to the wise among the people. Gradually, the term "apocrypha" took on a pejorative connotation, for the orthodoxy of these hidden books was often questionable. Origen (Comm. in Matt. 10.18; p. 13.881) distinguished between books that were to be read in public worship and apocryphal books. Because these secret books were often preserved for use within the esoteric circles of the divinely - knit believers, many of the critically - spirited or "unenlightened" Church Fathers found themselves outside the realm of understanding, and therefore came to apply the term "apocryphal" to, what they claimed to be, heretical works which were forbidden to be read.

In Protestant parlance, "the Apocrypha" designate 15 works, all but one of which are Jewish in origin and found in the Septuagint (parts of 2 Esdras are Christian and Latin in origin). Although some of them were composed in Palestine in Aramaic or Hebrew, they were not accepted into the Jewish canon formed late in the 2nd century AD (Canonicity, 67:31-35). The Reformers, influenced by the Jewish canon of the Old Testament, did not consider these books on a par with the rest of the Scriptures; thus the custom arose of making the Apocrypha a separate section in the Protestant Bible, or sometimes even of omitting them entirely (Canonicity, 67:44-46). The Catholic view, expressed as a doctrine of faith at the Council of Trent, is that 12 of these 15 works (in a different enumeration, however) are canonical Scripture; they are called the Deuterocanonical Books (Canonicity, 67:21, 42-43).

The three books of the Protestant Apocrypha that are not accepted by Catholics are 1-2 Esdras and the Prayer of Manasseh. The theme of the Book of Enoch dealing with the nature and deeds of the fallen angels so infuriated the later Church fathers that one, Filastrius, actually condemned it openly as heresy (Filastrius, Liber de Haeresibus, no. 108). Nor did the rabbis deign to give credence to the book's teaching about angels. Rabbi Simeon ben Jochai in the second century A.D. pronounced a curse upon those who believed it (Delitzsch, p. 223). So the book was denounced, banned, cursed, no doubt burned and shredded - and last but not least, lost (and conveniently forgotten) for a thousand years. But with an uncanny persistence, the Book of Enoch found its way back into circulation two centuries ago.

In 1773, rumors of a surviving copy of the book drew Scottish explorer James Bruce to distant Ethiopia. True to hearsay, the Book of Enoch had been preserved by the Ethiopic church, which put it right alongside the other books of the Bible. Bruce secured not one, but three Ethiopic copies of the book and brought them back to Europe and Britain. When in 1821 Dr. Richard Laurence, a Hebrew professor at Oxford, produced the first English translation of the work, the modern world gained its first glimpse of the forbidden mysteries of Enoch.

Most scholars say that the present form of the story in the Book of Enoch was penned sometime during the second century B.C. and was popular for at least five hundred years. The earliest Ethiopic text was apparently made from a Greek manuscript of the Book of Enoch, which itself was a copy of an earlier text. The original was apparently written in Semitic language, now thought to be Aramaic.

Though it was once believed to be post-Christian (the similarities to Christian terminology and teaching are striking), recent discoveries of copies of the book among the Dead Sea Scrolls found at Qumran prove that the book was in existence before the time of Jesus Christ. But the date of the original writing upon which the second century B.C. Qumran copies were based is shrouded in obscurity. It is, in a word, old. It has been largely the opinion of historians that the book does not really contain the authentic words of the ancient biblical patriarch Enoch, since he would have lived (based on the chronologies in the Book of Genesis) several thousand years earlier than the first known appearance of the book attributed to him. Although in the book he commands his son Methuselah to preserve the book unto future generations, which in itself is a call to copy the books he wrote so they might not be lost to the ages.

Despite its unknown origins, Christians once accepted the words of this Book of Enoch as authentic scripture, especially the part about the fallen angels and their prophesied judgment. In fact, many of the key concepts used by Jesus Christ himself seem directly connected to terms and ideas in the Book of Enoch. Thus, it is hard to avoid the conclusion that Jesus had not only studied the book, but also respected it highly enough to adopt and elaborate on its specific descriptions of the coming kingdom and its theme of inevitable judgment descending upon "the wicked" - the term most often used in the Old Testament to describe the Watchers.

There is abundant proof that Christ approved of the Book of Enoch. Over a hundred phrases in the New Testament find precedents in the Book of Enoch. Another remarkable bit of evidence for the early Christians' acceptance of the Book of Enoch was for many years buried under the King James Bible's mistranslation of Luke 9:35, describing the transfiguration of Christ: "And there came a voice out of the cloud, saying, 'This is my beloved Son: hear him." Apparently the translator here wished to make this verse agree with a similar verse in Matthew and Mark. But Luke's verse in the original Greek reads: "This is my Son, the Elect One (from the Greek ho eklelegmenos, lit., "the elect one"): hear him." The "Elect One" is a most significant term (found fourteen times) in the Book of Enoch. If the book was indeed known to the apostles of Christ, with its abundant descriptions of the Elect One who should "sit upon the throne of glory" and the Elect One who should "dwell in the midst of them," then the great scriptural authenticity is accorded to the Book of Enoch when the "voice out of the cloud" tells the apostles, "This is my Son, the Elect One" - the one promised in the Book of Enoch.

The Book of Jude tells us in verse 14 that "Enoch, the seventh from Adam, prophesied..." Jude also, in verse 15, makes a direct reference to the Book of Enoch (2:1), where he writes, "to execute judgment on all, to convict all who are ungodly..." The time difference between Enoch and Jude is approximately 3400 years. Therefore, Jude's reference to the Enoch's prophesies strongly leans toward the conclusion that these written prophesies were available to him at that time.

Fragments of ten Enoch manuscripts were found among the Dead Sea Scrolls. The famous scrolls actually comprise only one part of the total findings at Qumran. Much of the rest was Enochian literature, copies of the Book of Enoch, and other apocryphal works in the Enochian tradition, like the Book of Jubilees. With so many copies around, the Essenes could well have used the Enochian writings as a community prayer book or teacher's manual and study text.

The Book of Enoch was also used by writers of the non-canonical (i.e. apocryphal or "hidden") texts. The author of the apocryphal Epistle of Barnabas quotes the Book of Enoch three times, twice calling it "the Scripture," a term specifically denoting the inspired Word of God (Epis. of Barnabas 4:3, 16:5,6). Other apocryphal works reflect knowledge of the Enoch story of the Watchers, notably the Testaments of the Twelve Patriarchs and the Book of Jubilees.

Many of the early church fathers also supported the Enochian writings. Justin Martyr ascribed all evil to demons whom he alleged to be the offspring of the angels who fell through lust for women-directly referencing the Enochian writings. Athenagoras, writing in his work called Legatio in about 170 A.D., regards Enoch as a true prophet. He describes the angels which "violated both their own nature and their office." In his writings, he goes into detail about the nature of fallen angels and the cause of their fall, which comes directly from the Enochian writings.

Many other church fathers: Tatian (110-172); Irenaeus, Bishop of Lyons (115-185); Clement of Alexandria (150-220); Tertullian (160-230); Origen (186-255); Lactantius (260-330); in addition to: Methodius of Philippi, Minucius Felix, Commodianus, and Ambrose of Milanalso-also approved of and supported the Enochian writings.

The twentieth-century discovery of several Aramaic Enochian texts among the Dead Sea Scrolls prompted Catholic scholar J.T. Milik to compile a complete history of the Enochian writings, including translations of the Aramaic manuscripts. Milik's 400-page book, published in 1976 by Oxford (J. T. Milik, ed. and trans., The Books of Enoch: Aramaic Fragments of Qumran Cave 4, Oxford: Clarendon Press, 1976) is a milestone in Enochian scholarship, and Milik himself is no doubt one of the finest experts on the subject. His opinions, based as they are on years of in-depth research, are highly respected.

One by one the arguments against the Book of Enoch fade away. The day may soon arrive when the final complaints about the Book of Enoch's lack of historicity and "late date" are also silenced by new evidence of the book's real antiquity. Such evidence would be perhaps the return of Enoch, of whom there is no record of ever dying but rather still living in the Kingdom of Heaven. It is appointed unto man once to die, so Enoch has to die once in order for that Scripture to be fulfilled. Spiritual scholars have attributed the fulfillment of the prophecies of Enoch being revealed in Revelation 11 of which we find the return of Enoch with a second reprimand of the world for three and a half years. Wearing sackcloth and perhaps with Elijah for company - we may finally be able to account of his life and times after hearing what he has to say in those days to come - until we see him finally die, lay lifeless for three days and then rise up into the heavens yet again.

So, it goes without saying that I, Dr. Jay Winter, would standardize this glorious manuscript and distribute it for free. The message of the manuscript is too grand and celestial to have been penned solely by man. There is the work of God afoot within the text and you can sense it when you read it. For the last thousand years of mankind this book was blotted out of existence by many, yet a few who knew its importance preserved it for future generations. Translating the book into Ethiopic, a language that those who were persecuting the book did not understand. This saved the manuscript from the fires and is the primary reason that we have the book today. It is with my hope that the electronic version of this book reach as many as possible. As I write this in 2017, the ebook has reached more than 50,000 people free of charge. Distributing this text is my mission and I implore its readers to both study and share it with others. May God bless all who find this manuscript!

In the future, Biblical scholars say, that Enoch and Elijah will return to Earth to preach to the godless people of the world. When they do, remember their books and their history. It is important to understand that these two men through recorded history have never died. They've been alive for thousands of years preserved by the grace of God. Their destiny according to the books is to be slain by the Antichrist. This is the way that has been appointed unto them to die. They cannot die before then. As the prophecy in Revelations says, their bodies will lay in the streets for three days, then a voice from heaven will call them, their bodies will rise into the air as an earthquake kills $1/3^{rd}$ of the city. If you are alive when these things are happening, surely you must repent! But before they die, beware, flames go forth out of their mouths and consume those who would try to kill them. Repent! There is no other logical option!

Book 1
The Watchers

Chapter 1
The Words of the Blessing of Enoch

1 The words of the blessing of Enoch, wherewith he blessed the elect and righteous, who will be living in the days of tribulation, when all the wicked and godless are to be removed.

2 And Enoch, a righteous man whose eyes were opened by God took up his parable and said, "I saw the vision of the Holy One in the heavens, which the angels showed me, and from them I heard everything, and from them I understood as I saw, but not for this generation, but for a remote one which is for to come."

3 Concerning the elect I said, and took up my parable concerning them: "The Holy Great One will come forth from His dwelling,

4 And the eternal God will tread upon the earth, even on Mount Sinai and will appear in the strength of His might from the heaven of heavens.

5 And all shall be smitten with fear and the Watchers shall quake, and great fear and trembling shall seize them unto the ends of the earth.

6 And the high mountains shall be shaken and the high hills shall be made low, and shall melt like wax before the flame.

7 And the earth shall be wholly rent in sunder and all that is upon the earth shall perish, and there shall be a judgment upon all.

8 But with the righteous He will make peace. And will protect the elect, And mercy shall be upon them. And they shall all belong to God, And they shall be prospered, And they shall all be blessed. And He will help them all, And light shall appear unto them, And He will make peace with them.

9 And behold! He cometh with ten thousands of His holy ones to execute judgment upon all, And to destroy all the ungodly: And to convict all flesh Of all the works of their ungodliness which they have ungodly committed, And of all the hard things which ungodly sinners have spoken against Him."

Chapter 2
The Creation

1 Observe ye everything that takes place in the heaven, how they do not change their orbits, and the luminaries which are in the heaven, how they all rise and set in order each in its season, and transgress not against their appointed order.

2 Behold ye the earth, and give heed to the things which take place upon it from first to last, how steadfast they are, how none of the things upon earth change, but all the works of God appear to you. Behold the summer and the winter, how the whole earth is filled with water, and clouds and dew and rain lie upon it.

3 Observe and see how in the winter all the trees seem as though they had withered and shed all their leaves, except fourteen trees, which do not lose their foliage but retain the old foliage from two to three years till the new comes.

4 And again, observe ye the days of summer how the sun is above the earth over against it. And you seek shade and shelter by reason of the heat of the sun, and the earth also burns with growing heat, and so you cannot tread on the earth, or on a rock by reason of its heat.

5 Observe ye how the trees cover themselves with green leaves and bear fruit: wherefore give ye heed and know with regard to all His works, and recognize how He that liveth for ever hath made them so.

6 And all His works go on thus from year to year for ever, and all the tasks which they accomplish for Him, and their tasks change not, but according as God hath ordained so is it done.

7 And behold how the sea and the rivers in like manner accomplish and change not their tasks from His commandments.

8 But ye have not been steadfast, nor done the commandments of the Lord, But ye have turned away and spoken proud and hard words With your impure mouths against His greatness. Oh, ye hard hearted, ye shall find no peace.

9 Therefore shall ye execrate your days, and the years of your life shall perish, and the years of your destruction shall be multiplied in eternal abomination, and ye shall find no mercy.

10 In those days ye shall make your names an eternal abomination unto all the righteous, and by you shall all who curse, curse. All the sinners and godless shall imprecate by you. And for you, the godless there shall be a curse."

11 And all the righteous shall rejoice, and there shall be forgiveness of sins, and every mercy and peace and forbearance.

12 There shall be salvation unto them, a goodly light.

13 And for all of you sinners there shall be no salvation but on you all shall abide the curse of the beast.

14 But for the elect there shall be light and joy and peace, and they shall inherit the earth.

15 And then there shall be bestowed upon the elect wisdom, and they shall all live and never again sin either through ungodliness or through pride: But they who are wise shall be humble.

16 And they shall not again transgress, nor shall they sin all the days of their life, nor shall they die of anger or wrath but they shall complete the number of the days of their life.

17 And their lives shall be increased in peace, and the years of their joy shall be multiplied in eternal gladness and peace all the days of their life.

Chapter 3
Fallen Angels

1 And it came to pass when the children of men had multiplied that in those days were born unto them beautiful and comely daughters.

2 And the angels, the children of the heaven, saw and lusted after them, and said to one another: "Come, let us choose us wives from among the children of men and beget us children."

3 And Semjaza, who was their leader, said unto them: "I fear ye will not indeed agree to do this deed, and I alone shall have to pay the penalty of a great sin."

4 And they all answered him and said: "Let us all swear an oath, and all bind ourselves by mutual imprecations not to abandon this plan but to do this thing."

5 Then sware they all together and bound themselves by mutual imprecations upon it. And they were in all two hundred; who descended in the days of Jared on the summit of Mount Hermon, and they called it Mount Hermon, because they had sworn and bound themselves by mutual imprecations upon it.

6 And these are the names of their leaders: Samlazaz, their leader, Araklba, Rameel, Kokablel, Tamlel, Ramlel, Danel, Ezeqeel, Baraqijal, Asael, Armaros, Batarel, Ananel, Zaqlel, Samsapeel, Satarel, Turel, Jomjael, Sariel. These are their chiefs of tens.

7 And all the others together with them took unto themselves wives, and each chose for himself one, and they began to go in unto them and to defile themselves with them.

8 And they taught them charms and enchantments, and the cutting of roots, and made them acquainted with plants.

9 And they became pregnant, and they bare great giants, whose height was three thousand ells: Who consumed all the acquisitions of men. And when men could no longer sustain them, the giants turned against them and devoured mankind.

10 And they began to sin against birds, and beasts, and reptiles, and fish, and to devour one another's flesh, and drink the blood. Then the earth laid accusation against the lawless ones.

11 And Azazel taught men to make swords, and knives, and shields, and breastplates, and made known to them the metals of the earth and the art of working them, and bracelets, and ornaments, and the use of antimony, and the beautifying of the eyelids, and all kinds of costly stones, and all colouring tinctures.

12 And there arose much godlessness, and they committed fornication, and they were led astray, and became corrupt in all their ways.

13 Semjaza taught enchantments and root cuttings, Armaros the resolving of enchantments, Baraqijal taught astrology, Kokabel the constellations, Ezeqeel the knowledge of the clouds, Araqiel the signs of the earth, Shamsiel the signs of the sun, and Sariel the course of the moon.

14 And as men perished, they cried, and their cry went up to heaven.

Chapter 4
Intercession of Angels

1 And then Michael, Uriel, Raphael, and Gabriel looked down from heaven and saw much blood being shed upon the earth, and all lawlessness being wrought upon the earth.

2 And they said one to another, "The earth made without inhabitant cries the voice of their cryingst up to the gates of heaven."

3 And now to you, the holy ones of heaven, the souls of men make their suit, saying, "Bring our cause before the Most High."

4 And they said to the Lord of the ages, "Lord of lords, God of gods, King of kings, and God of the ages, the throne of Thy glory standeth unto all the generations of the ages, and Thy name holy and glorious and blessed unto all the ages! Thou hast made all things, and power over all things hast Thou, and all things are naked and open in Thy sight, and Thou seest all things, and nothing can hide itself from Thee.

5 Thou seest what Azazel hath done, who hath taught all unrighteousness on earth and revealed the eternal secrets which were in heaven, which men were striving to learn; and Samlazaz, to whom Thou hast given authority to bear rule over his associates.

6 And they have gone to the daughters of men upon the earth, and have slept with the women, and have defiled themselves, and revealed to them all kinds of sins. And the women have borne giants, and the whole earth has thereby been filled with blood and unrighteousness.

7 And now, behold, the souls of those who have died are crying out making their suit to the gates of heaven, and their lamentations have ascended and cannot cease because of the lawless deeds which are wrought on the earth.

8 And Thou knowest all things before they come to pass, and Thou seest these things and Thou dost suffer them, and Thou dost not say to us what we are to do to them in regard to these."

9 Then said the Most High, the Holy and Great One spake, and sent Uriel to the son of Lamech and said to him, "Go to Noah and tell him in my name 'Hide thyself!' and reveal to him the end that is approaching, that the whole earth will

be destroyed, and a deluge is about to come upon the whole earth, and will destroy all that is on it. And now instruct him that he may escape and his seed may be preserved for all the generations of the world."

10 And again the Lord said to Raphael, "Bind Azazel hand and foot, and cast him into the darkness: and make an opening in the desert, which is in Dudael, and cast him therein. And place upon him rough and jagged rocks, and cover him with darkness, and let him abide there for ever, and cover his face that he may not see light. And on the day of the great judgement he shall be cast into the fire.

11 And heal the earth which the angels have corrupted, and proclaim the healing of the earth, that they may heal the plague, and that all the children of men may not perish through all the secret things that the Watchers have disclosed and have taught their sons. And the whole earth has been corrupted through the works that were taught by Azazel, to him ascribe all sin."

12 And to Gabriel said the Lord, "Proceed against the bastards and the reprobates, and against the children of fornication and destroy the children of the Watchers from amongst men. Send them one against the other that they may destroy each other in battle, for length of days shall they not have. And no request that they make of thee shall be granted unto their fathers on their behalf; for they hope to live an eternal life, and that each one of them will live five hundred years."

13 And the Lord said unto Michael, "Go, bind Samlazaz and his associates who have united themselves with women so as to have defiled themselves with them in all their uncleanness. And when their sons have slain one another, and they have seen the destruction of their beloved ones, bind them fast for seventy generations in the valleys of the earth, till the day of their judgement and of their consummation, till the judgement that is for ever and ever is consummated. In those days they shall be led off to the abyss of fire and to the torment and the prison in which they shall be confined for ever.

14 And whosoever shall be condemned and destroyed will from thenceforth be bound together with them to the end of all generations. and destroy all the spirits of the reprobate and the children of the Watchers because they have wronged mankind.

15 Destroy all wrong from the face of the earth and let every evil work come to an end, and let the plant of righteousness and truth appear, and it shall prove a blessing; the works of righteousness and truth shall be planted in truth and joy for evermore.

16 And then shall all the righteous escape and shall live till they beget thousands of children, and all the days of their youth and their old age shall they complete in peace.

17 And then shall the whole earth be tilled in righteousness, and shall all be planted with trees and be full of blessing.

18 And all desirable trees shall be planted on it, and they shall plant vines on it and the vine which they plant thereon shall yield wine in abundance, and as for all the seed which is sown thereon each measure shall bear a thousand, and each measure of olives shall yield ten presses of oil.

19 And cleanse thou the earth from all oppression, and from all unrighteousness, and from all sin, and from all godlessness, and all the uncleanness that is wrought upon the earth destroy from off the earth.

20 And all the children of men shall become righteous, and all nations shall offer adoration and shall praise Me, and all shall worship Me. And the earth shall be cleansed from all defilement, and from all sin, and from all punishment, and from all torment, and I will never again send upon it from generation to generation and for ever.

21 And in those days I will open the store chambers of blessing which are in the heaven, so as to send them down upon the earth over the work and labour of the children of men. And truth and peace shall be associated together throughout all the days of the world and throughout all the generations of men."

22 Before these things Enoch was hidden, and no one of the children of men knew where he was hidden, and where he abode, and what had become of him. And his activities had to do with the Watchers, and his days were with the holy ones.

23 And I Enoch was blessing the Lord of Majesty and the King of the ages, and lo! the Watchers called me, Enoch the scribe, and said to me: "Enoch, thou scribe of righteousness, go, declare to the Watchers of the heaven who have left the high heaven, the holy eternal place, and have defiled themselves with women, and have done as the children of earth do, and have taken unto themselves wives.

24 Say to them: 'Ye have wrought great destruction on the earth and ye shall have no peace nor forgiveness of sin.'

25 And inasmuch as they delight themselves in their children the murder of their beloved ones shall they see, and over the destruction of their children shall they

lament, and shall make supplication unto eternity, but mercy and peace shall ye not attain."

26 And Enoch went and said: "Azazel, thou shalt have no peace, a severe sentence has gone forth against thee to put thee in bonds and thou shalt not have toleration nor request granted to thee, because of the unrighteousness which thou hast taught, and because of all the works of godlessness and unrighteousness and sin which thou hast shown to men."

27 Then I went and spoke to them all together, and they were all afraid, and fear and trembling seized them. And they besought me to draw up a petition for them that they might find forgiveness, and to read their petition in the presence of the Lord of heaven.

28 For from thenceforward they could not speak with Him nor lift up their eyes to heaven for shame of their sins for which they had been condemned.

29 Then I wrote out their petition, and the prayer in regard to their spirits and their deeds individually and in regard to their requests that they should have forgiveness and length.

30 And I went off and sat down at the waters of Dan, in the land of Dan, to the south of the west of Hermon, I read their petition till I fell asleep.

31 And behold a dream came to me, and visions fell down upon me, and I saw visions of chastisement, and a voice came bidding me to tell it to the sons of heaven, and reprimand them.

32 And when I awaked, I came unto them, and they were all sitting gathered together, weeping in Abelsjail, which is between Lebanon and Seneser, with their faces covered.

33 And I recounted before them all the visions which I had seen in sleep, and I began to speak the words of righteousness, and to reprimand the heavenly Watchers.

Chapter 5
Book of the Words of Righteousness

1 The book of the words of righteousness, and of the reprimand of the eternal Watchers in accordance with the command of the Holy Great One in that vision I saw in my sleep.

2 What I will now say with a tongue of flesh and with the breath of my mouth, which the Great One has given to men to converse therewith and understand with the heart.

3 As He has created and given to man the power of understanding the word of wisdom, so hath He created me also and given me the power of reprimanding the Watchers, the children of heaven.

4 "I wrote out your petition, and in my vision it appeared thus, that your petition will not be granted unto you throughout all the days of eternity, and that judgement has been finally passed upon you.

5 Your petition will not be granted unto you. And from henceforth you shall not ascend into heaven unto all eternity, and in bonds of the earth the decree has gone forth to bind you for all the days of the world.

6 And previously you shall have seen the destruction of your beloved sons and ye shall have no pleasure in them, but they shall fall before you by the sword.

7 And your petition on their behalf shall not be granted, nor yet on your own even though you weep and pray and speak all the words contained in the writing which I have written.

8 And the vision was shown to me thus: Behold, in the vision clouds invited me and a mist summoned me, and the course of the stars and the lightnings sped and hastened me, and the winds in the vision caused me to fly and lifted me upward, and bore me into heaven.

9 And I went in till I drew nigh to a wall which is built of crystals and surrounded by tongues of fire: and it began to affright me.

10 And I went into the tongues of fire and drew nigh to a large house which was built of crystals and the walls of the house were like a tesselated floor made of crystals, and its groundwork was of crystal.

11 Its ceiling was like the path of the stars and the lightnings, and between them were fiery cherubim, and their heaven was water.

12 A flaming fire surrounded the walls, and its portals blazed with fire.

13 And I entered into that house, and it was hot as fire and cold as ice. There were no delights of life therein; fear covered me, and trembling got hold upon me.

14 And as I quaked and trembled, I fell upon my face and I beheld a vision, and lo! there was a second house, greater than the former, and the entire portal stood open before me, and it was built of flames of fire.

15 And in every respect it so excelled in splendor and magnificence and extent that I cannot describe to you its splendor and its extent.

16 And its floor was of fire, and above it were lightnings and the path of the stars, and its ceiling also was flaming fire. And I looked and saw therein a lofty throne, its appearance was as crystal, and the wheels thereof as the shining sun, and there was the vision of cherubim.

17 And from underneath the throne came streams of flaming fire so that I could not look thereon.

18 And the Great Glory sat thereon, and His raiment shone more brightly than the sun and was whiter than any snow.

19 None of the angels could enter and could behold His face by reason of the magnificence and glory and no flesh could behold Him.

20 The flaming fire was round about Him, and a great fire stood before Him, and none around could draw nigh Him; ten thousand times ten thousand were before Him, yet He needed no counselor.

21 And the most holy ones who were nigh to Him did not leave by night nor depart from Him. And until then I had been prostrate on my face, trembling and the Lord called me with His own mouth, and said to me: "Come hither, Enoch, and hear my word."

22 And one of the holy ones came to me and waked me, and He made me rise up and approach the door, and I bowed my face downwards.

23 And He answered and said to me, and I heard His voice: "Fear not, Enoch, thou righteous man and scribe of righteousness. Approach hither and hear my voice.

24 And go, say to the Watchers of heaven, who have sent thee to intercede for them: 'You should intercede for men, and not men for you. Wherefore have ye left the high, holy, and eternal heaven, and lain with women, and defiled yourselves with the daughters of men and taken to yourselves wives, and done like the children of earth, and begotten giants as your sons.

25 And though ye were holy, spiritual, living the eternal life, you have defiled yourselves with the blood of women, and have begotten with the blood of flesh, and, as the children of men, have lusted after flesh and blood as those also do who die and perish.

26 Therefore have I given them wives also that they might impregnate them, and beget children by them, that thus nothing might be wanting to them on earth.

27 But you were formerly spiritual, living the eternal life, and immortal for all generations of the world. And therefore I have not appointed wives for you; for as for the spiritual ones of the heaven, in heaven is their dwelling.

28 And now, the giants, who are produced from the spirits and flesh, shall be called evil spirits upon the earth, and on the earth shall be their dwelling.

29 Evil spirits have proceeded from their bodies; because they are born from men and from the Watchers is their beginning and primal origin; they shall be evil spirits on earth, and evil spirits shall they be called.

30 And the spirits of the giants afflict, oppress, destroy, attack, do battle, and work destruction on the earth, and cause trouble. They take no food, but nevertheless hunger and thirst, and cause offences.

31 And these spirits shall rise up against the children of men and against the women, because they have proceeded from them.

32 From the days of the slaughter and destruction and death of the giants, from the souls of whose flesh the spirits, having gone forth, shall destroy without incurring judgement, thus shall they destroy until the day of the consummation, the great judgement in which the age shall be consummated, over the Watchers and the godless, yea, shall be wholly consummated.

33 And now as to the Watchers who have sent thee to intercede for them, who had been aforetime in heaven, say to them: "You have been in heaven, but all the mysteries had not yet been revealed to you, and you knew worthless ones, and these in the hardness of your hearts you have made known to the women, and through these mysteries women and men work much evil on earth."

34 Say to them therefore: "You have no peace."

Chapter 6
Taken by Angels

1 Angels took and brought me to a place in which those who were there were like flaming fire, and when they wished, they appeared as men.

2 And they brought me to the place of darkness, and to a mountain the point of whose summit reached to heaven.

3 And I saw the places of the luminaries and the treasuries of the stars and of the thunder and in the uttermost depths, where were a fiery bow and arrows and their quiver, and a fiery sword and all the lightnings.

4 And they took me to the living waters, and to the fire of the west, which receives every setting of the sun.

5 And I came to a river of fire in which the fire flows like water and discharges itself into the great sea towards the west.

6 I saw the great rivers and came to the great river and to the great darkness, and went to the place where no flesh walks. I saw the mountains of the darkness of winter and the place whence all the waters of the deep flow.

7 I saw the mouths of all the rivers of the earth and the mouth of the deep.

8 I saw the treasuries of all the winds, I saw how He had furnished with them the whole creation and the firm foundations of the earth.

9 And I saw the corner stone of the earth, I saw the four winds which bear the firmament of the heaven.

10 And I saw how the winds stretch out the vaults of heaven, and have their station between heaven and earth: these are the pillars of the heaven.

11 I saw the winds of heaven which turn and bring the circumference of the sun and all the stars to their setting.

12 I saw the winds on the earth carrying the clouds: I saw the paths of the angels.

13 I saw at the end of the earth the firmament of the heaven above and I proceeded and saw a place which burns day and night, where there are seven mountains of magnificent stones.

14 Three towards the east, and three towards the south. And as for those towards the east, was of coloured stone, and one of pearl, and one of jacinth, and those towards the south of red stone.

15 But the middle one reached to heaven like the throne of God, of alabaster, and the summit of the throne was of sapphire.

16 And I saw a flaming fire. And beyond these mountains is a region the end of the great earth: there the heavens were completed.

17 And I saw a deep abyss, with columns of heavenly fire, and among them I saw columns of fire fall, which were beyond measure alike towards the height and towards the depth.

18 And beyond that abyss I saw a place which had no firmament of the heaven above, and no firmly founded earth beneath it: there was no water upon it, and no birds, but it was a waste and horrible place.

19 I saw there seven stars like great burning mountains, and to me, when I inquired regarding them. The angel said: "This place is the end of heaven and earth. This has become a prison for the stars and the host of heaven.

20 And the stars which roll over the fire are they which have transgressed the commandment of the Lord in the beginning of their rising, because they did not come forth at their appointed times.

21 And He was wroth with them, and bound them till the time when their guilt should be consummated for ten thousand years."

22 And Uriel said to me: "Here shall stand the angels who have connected themselves with women, and their spirits assuming many different forms are defiling mankind and shall lead them astray into sacrificing to demons as gods.

23 Here shall they stand, till the day of the great judgement in which they shall be judged till they are made an end of. And the women also of the angels who went astray shall become sirens."

24 And I, Enoch, alone saw the vision, the ends of all things: and no man shall see as I have seen.

Chapter 7
The Holy Angels

1 And these are the names of the holy angels who watch mankind.

2 Uriel, one of the holy angels, who is over the world and over Tartarus.

3 Raphael, one of the holy angels, who is over the spirits of men.

4 Raguel, one of the holy angels who takes vengeance on the world of the luminaries.

5 Michael, one of the holy angels, to wit, he that is set over the best part of mankind and over chaos.

6 Saraqael, one of the holy angels, who is set over the spirits, who sin in the spirit.

7 Gabriel, one of the holy angels, who is over Paradise and the serpents and the Cherubim.

8 Remiel, one of the holy angels, whom God set over those who rise.

9 And I proceeded to where things were chaotic. And I saw there something horrible: I saw neither a heaven above nor a firmly founded earth, but a place chaotic and horrible.

10 And there I saw seven stars of the heaven bound together in it, like great mountains and burning with fire.

11 Then I said: "For what sin are they bound, and on what account have they been cast in hither?"

12 Then said Uriel, one of the holy angels, who was with me, and was chief over them, and said: "Enoch, why dost thou ask, and why art thou eager for the truth? These are of the number of the stars of heaven, which have transgressed the commandment of the Lord, and are bound here till ten thousand years, the time entailed by their sins, are consummated."

13 And from thence I went to another place, which was still more horrible than the former, and I saw a horrible thing. A great fire there which burnt and blazed,

and the place was cleft as far as the abyss, being full of great descending columns of fire. Neither its extent or magnitude could I see, nor could I conjecture.

14 Then I said: "How fearful is the place and how terrible to look upon!"

15 Then Uriel answered me, one of the holy angels who was with me, and said unto me: "Enoch, why hast thou such fear and affright?"

16 And I answered: "Because of this fearful place, and because of the spectacle of the pain."

17 And he said unto me: "This place is the prison of the angels, and here they will be imprisoned for ever."

18 And thence I went to another place, the mountain of hard rock.

19 And there was in it four hollow places, deep and wide and very smooth. How smooth are the hollow places and deep and dark to look at.

20 Then Raphael answered, one of the holy angels who was with me, and said unto me: "These hollow places have been created for this very purpose, that the spirits of the souls of the dead should assemble therein, yea that all the souls of the children of men should assemble here. And these places have been made to receive them till the day of their judgement and till their appointed period, till the great judgement upon them."

21 I saw a dead man making suit, and his voice went forth to heaven and made suit. And I asked Raphael the angel who was with me, and I said unto him: "This spirit which maketh suit, whose is it, whose voice goeth forth and maketh suit to heaven?"

22 And he answered me saying: "This is the spirit which went forth from Abel, whom his brother Cain slew, and he makes his suit against him till his seed is destroyed from the face of the earth, and his seed is annihilated from amongst the seed of men."

23 The I asked regarding it, and regarding all the hollow places: "Why is one separated from the other?"

24 And he answered me and said unto me: "These three have been made that the spirits of the dead might be separated. And such a division has been make for the spirits of the righteous, in which there is the bright spring of water. And such has

been made for sinners when they die and are buried in the earth and judgement has not been executed on them in their lifetime.

25 Here their spirits shall be set apart in this great pain till the great day of judgement and punishment and torment of those who curse for ever and retribution for their spirits. There He shall bind them for ever. And such a division has been made for the spirits of those who make their suit, who make disclosures concerning their destruction, when they were slain in the days of the sinners.

26 Such has been made for the spirits of men who were not righteous but sinners, who were complete in transgression, and of the transgressors they shall be companions but their spirits shall not be slain in the day of judgement nor shall they be raised from thence."

27 The I blessed the Lord of glory and said: "Blessed be my Lord, the Lord of righteousness, who ruleth for ever."

28 From thence I went to another place to the west of the ends of the earth. And I saw a burning fire which ran without resting, and paused not from its course day or night but regularly.

29 And I asked saying: "What is this which rests not?"

30 Then Raguel, one of the holy angels who was with me, answered me and said unto me: "This course of fire which thou hast seen is the fire in the west which persecutes all the luminaries of heaven."

31 And from thence I went to another place of the earth, and he showed me a mountain range of fire which burnt day and night.

32 And I went beyond it and saw seven magnificent mountains all differing each from the other, and the stones were magnificent and beautiful, magnificent as a whole, of glorious appearance and fair exterior: three towards the east, one founded on the other, and three towards the south, one upon the other, and deep rough ravines, no one of which joined with any other.

33 And the seventh mountain was in the midst of these, and it excelled them in height, resembling the seat of a throne: and fragrant trees encircled the throne.

34 And amongst them was a tree such as I had never yet smelt, neither was any amongst them nor were others like it: it had a fragrance beyond all fragrance, and

its leaves and blooms and wood wither not for ever: and its fruit is beautiful, and its fruit resembles the dates of a palm.

35 Then I said: "How beautiful is this tree, and fragrant, and its leaves are fair, and its blooms very delightful in appearance."

36 Then answered Michael, one of the holy and honored angels who was with me, and was their leader.

37 And he said unto me: "Enoch, why dost thou ask me regarding the fragrance of the tree, and why dost thou wish to learn the truth?"

38 Then I answered him saying: "I wish to know about everything, but especially about this tree."

39 And he answered saying: "This high mountain which thou hast seen, whose summit is like the throne of God, is His throne, where the Holy Great One, the Lord of Glory, the Eternal King, will sit, when He shall come down to visit the earth with goodness. And as for this fragrant tree no mortal is permitted to touch it till the great judgement, when He shall take vengeance on all and bring to its consummation for ever. It shall then be given to the righteous and holy. Its fruit shall be for food to the elect: it shall be transplanted to the holy place, to the temple of the Lord, the Eternal King.

40 Then shall they rejoice with joy and be glad, and into the holy place shall they enter; and its fragrance shall be in their bones, and they shall live a long life on earth. Such as thy fathers lived; and in their days shall no sorrow or plague or torment or calamity touch them."

41 Then blessed I the God of Glory, the Eternal King, who hath prepared such things for the righteous, and hath created them and promised to give to them.

42 And I went from thence to the middle of the earth, and I saw a blessed place in which there were trees with branches abiding and blooming.

43 And there I saw a holy mountain, and underneath the mountain to the east there was a stream and it flowed towards the south. And I saw towards the east another mountain higher than this, and between them a deep and narrow ravine: in it also ran a stream underneath the mountain.

44 And to the west thereof there was another mountain, lower than the former and of small elevation, and a ravine deep and dry between them: and another deep and dry ravine was at the extremities of the three mountains.

45 And all the ravines were deep and narrow, of hard rock, and trees were not planted upon them. And I marveled at the rocks, and I marveled at the ravine, yea, I marveled very much.

46 Then said I: "For what object is this blessed land, which is entirely filled with trees, and this accursed valley between?"

47 Then Uriel, one of the holy angels who was with me, answered and said: "This accursed valley is for those who are accursed for ever. Here shall all the accursed be gathered together who utter with their lips against the Lord unseemly words and of His glory speak hard things. Here shall they be gathered together, and here shall be their place of judgement.

48 In the last days there shall be upon them the spectacle of righteous judgement in the presence of the righteous for ever: here shall the merciful bless the Lord of glory, the Eternal King. In the days of judgement over the former, they shall bless Him for the mercy in accordance with which He has assigned them."

49 Then I blessed the Lord of Glory and set forth His glory and lauded Him gloriously.

50 And thence I went towards the east, into the midst of the mountain range of the desert, and I saw a wilderness and it was solitary, full of trees and plants. And water gushed forth from above. Rushing like a copious watercourse towards the north west it caused clouds and dew to ascend on every side.

51 And thence I went to another place in the desert, and approached to the east of this mountain range. And there I saw aromatic trees exhaling the fragrance of frankincense and myrrh, and the trees also were similar to the almond tree.

52 And beyond these, I went afar to the east, and I saw another place, a valley of water. And therein there was a tree, the color of fragrant trees such as the mastic. And on the sides of those valleys I saw fragrant cinnamon. And beyond these I proceeded to the east.

53 And I saw other mountains, and amongst them were groves of trees, and there flowed forth from them nectar, which is named sarara and galbanum. And beyond these mountains I saw another mountain to the east of the ends of the earth, whereon were aloe trees, and all the trees were full of stacte, being like almond trees. And when one burnt it, it smelt sweeter than any fragrant odour.

54 And after these fragrant odours, as I looked towards the north over the mountains I saw seven mountains full of choice nard and fragrant trees and cinnamon and pepper.

55 And thence I went over the summits of all these mountains, far towards the east of the earth, and passed above the Erythraean sea and went far from it, and passed over the angel Zotiel.

56 And I came to the Garden of Righteousness, and from afar off I saw numerous trees, and these great two trees there, very great, beautiful, and glorious, and magnificent, and the Tree of Knowledge, whose holy fruit they eat and know great wisdom.

57 That tree is in height like the strangler fig, and its leaves are like the Carob tree, and its fruit is like the clusters of the vine, very beautiful: and the fragrance of the tree penetrates afar.

58 Then I said: "How beautiful is the tree, and how attractive is its look!"

59 Then Raphael the holy angel, who was with me, answered me and said: "This is the tree of wisdom, of which thy father old and thy aged mother, who were before thee, have eaten, and they learnt wisdom and their eyes were opened, and they knew that they were naked and they were driven out of the garden."

60 And from thence I went to the ends of the earth and saw there great beasts, and each differed from the other; and birds also differing in appearance and beauty and voice, the one differing from the other.

61 And to the east of those beasts I saw the ends of the earth whereon the heaven rests, and the portals of the heaven open. And I saw how the stars of heaven come forth, and I counted the portals out of which they proceed, and wrote down all their outlets, of each individual star by itself, according to their number and their names, their courses and their positions, and their times and their months, as Uriel the holy angel who was with me showed me.

62 He showed all things to me and wrote them down for me; also their names he wrote for me, and their laws and their companies.

63 And from thence I went towards the north to the ends of the earth, and there I saw a great and glorious device at the ends of the whole earth.

64 And here I saw three portals of heaven open in the heaven: through each of them proceed north winds: when they blow there is cold, hail, frost, snow, dew,

and rain. And out of one portal they blow for good: but when they blow through the other two portals, it is with violence and affliction on the earth, and they blow with violence.

65 And from thence I went towards the west to the ends of the earth, and saw there three portals of the heaven open such as I had seen in the east, the same number of portals, and the same number of outlets.

66 And from thence I went to the south to the ends of the earth, and saw there three open portals of the heaven: and thence there come dew, rain, and wind. And from thence I went to the east to the ends of the heaven, and saw here the three eastern portals of heaven open and small portals above them.

67 Through each of these small portals pass the stars of heaven and run their course to the west on the path which is shown to them.

68 And as often as I saw I blessed always the Lord of Glory, and I continued to bless the Lord of Glory who has wrought great and glorious wonders, to show the greatness of His work to the angels and to spirits and to men, that they might praise His work and all His creation: that they might see the work of His might and praise the great work of His hands and bless Him for ever.

Book 2
The Parables

Chapter 1
The First Parable

1 The second vision which he saw, the vision of wisdom, which Enoch the son of Jared, the son of Mahalaleel, the son of Cainan, the son of Enos, the son of Seth, the son of Adam, saw.

2 And this is the beginning of the words of wisdom which I lifted up my voice to speak and say to those which dwell on earth: "Hear, ye men of old time, and see, ye that come after, the words of the Holy One which I will speak before the Lord of Spirits. It were better to declare to the men of old times, but even from those that come after we will not withhold the beginning of wisdom."

3 Till the present day such wisdom has never been given by the Lord of Spirits as I have received according to my insight, according to the good pleasure of the Lord of Spirits by whom the lot of eternal life has been given to me. Now three Parables were imparted to me, and I lifted up my voice and recounted them to those that dwell on the earth.

4 The first Parable.
When the congregation of the righteous shall appear, and sinners shall be judged for their sins, and shall be driven from the face of the earth:

5 And when the Righteous One shall appear before the eyes of the righteous, whose elect works hang upon the Lord of Spirits, and light shall appear to the righteous and the elect who dwell on the earth, where then will be the dwelling of the sinners, and where the resting place of those who have denied the Lord of Spirits? It had been good for them if they had not been born.

6 When the secrets of the righteous shall be revealed and the sinners judged, and the godless driven from the presence of the righteous and elect.

7 From that time those that possess the earth shall no longer be powerful and exalted: And they shall not be able to behold the face of the holy, for the Lord of Spirits has caused His light to appear on the face of the holy, righteous, and elect.

8 Then shall the kings and the mighty perish and be given into the hands of the righteous and holy.

9 And thenceforward none shall seek for themselves mercy from the Lord of Spirits for their life is at an end.

10 And it shall come to pass in those days that elect and holy children will descend from the high heaven, and their seed will become one with the children of men.

11 And in those days Enoch received books of zeal and wrath, and books of disquiet and expulsion.

12 And mercy shall not be accorded to them, saith the Lord of Spirits.

13 And in those days a whirlwind carried me off from the earth, and set me down at the end of the heavens.

14 And there I saw another vision, the dwelling places of the holy, and the resting places of the righteous.

15 Here mine eyes saw their dwellings with His righteous angels and their resting places with the holy.

16 And they petitioned and interceded and prayed for the children of men, and righteousness flowed before them as water, and mercy like dew upon the earth: Thus it is amongst them for ever and ever.

17 And in that place mine eyes saw the Elect One of righteousness and of faith, and I saw his dwelling place under the wings of the Lord of Spirits.

18 And righteousness shall prevail in his days, and the righteous and elect shall be without number before Him for ever and ever.

19 And all the righteous and elect before Him shall be strong as fiery lights, and their mouth shall be full of blessing, and their lips extol the name of the Lord of Spirits, and righteousness before Him shall never fail.

20 There I wished to dwell, and my spirit longed for that dwelling place, and there heretofore hath been my portion. For so has it been established concerning me before the Lord of Spirits.

21 In those days I praised and extolled the name of the Lord of Spirits with blessings and praises, because He hath destined me for blessing and glory according to the good pleasure of the Lord of Spirits.

22 For a long time my eyes regarded that place, and I blessed Him and praised Him, saying: "Blessed is He, and may He be blessed from the beginning and for

evermore. And before Him there is no ceasing. He knows before the world was created what is for ever and what will be from generation unto generation."

23 Those who sleep not bless Thee: they stand before Thy glory and bless, praise, and extol, saying: "Holy, holy, holy, is the Lord of Spirits: He filleth the earth with spirits."

24 And here my eyes saw all those who sleep not: they stand before Him and bless and say: "Blessed be Thou, and blessed be the name of the Lord for ever and ever." And my face was changed; for I could no longer behold.

25 And after that I saw thousands of thousands and ten thousand times ten thousand, I saw a multitude beyond number and reckoning, who stood before the Lord of Spirits.

26 And on the four sides of the Lord of Spirits I saw four presences, different from those that sleep not, and I learnt their names: for the angel that went with me made known to me their names, and showed me all the hidden things.

27 And I heard the voices of those four presences as they uttered praises before the Lord of glory.

28 The first voice blesses the Lord of Spirits for ever and ever.

29 And the second voice I heard blessing the Elect One and the elect ones who hang upon the Lord of Spirits.

30 And the third voice I heard pray and intercede for those who dwell on the earth and supplicate in the name of the Lord of Spirits.

31 And I heard the fourth voice fending off the Satans and forbidding them to come before the Lord of Spirits to accuse them who dwell on the earth.

32 After that I asked the angel of peace who went with me, who showed me everything that is hidden: "Who are these four presences which I have seen and whose words I have heard and written down?"

33 And he said to me: "This first is Michael, the merciful and long suffering: and the second, who is set over all the diseases and all the wounds of the children of men, is Raphael: and the third, who is set over all the powers, is Gabriel: and the fourth, who is set over the repentance unto hope of those who inherit eternal life, is named Phanuel."

34 And these are the four angels of the Lord of Spirits and the four voices I heard in those days.

35 And after that I saw all the secrets of the heavens, and how the kingdom is divided, and how the actions of men are weighed in the balance.

36 And there I saw the mansions of the elect and the mansions of the holy, and mine eyes saw there all the sinners being driven from thence which deny the name of the Lord of Spirits, and being dragged off: and they could not abide because of the punishment which proceeds from the Lord of Spirits.

37 And there mine eyes saw the secrets of the lightning and of the thunder, and the secrets of the winds, how they are divided to blow over the earth, and the secrets of the clouds and dew, and these I saw from whence they proceed in that place and from whence they saturate the dusty earth.

38 And there I saw closed chambers out of which the winds are divided, the chamber of the hail and winds, the chamber of the mist, and of the clouds, and the cloud thereof hovers over the earth from the beginning of the world.

39 And I saw the chambers of the sun and moon, whence they proceed and whither they come again, and their glorious return, and how one is superior to the other, and their stately orbit, and how they do not leave their orbit, and they add nothing to their orbit and they take nothing from it, and they keep faith with each other, in accordance with the oath by which they are bound together.

40 And first the sun goes forth and traverses his path according to the commandment of the Lord of Spirits, and mighty is His name for ever and ever.

41 And after that I saw the hidden and the visible path of the moon, and she accomplishes the course of her path in that place by day and by night the one holding a position opposite to the other before the Lord of Spirits.

42 And they give thanks and praise and rest not. For unto them is their thanksgiving rest.

43 For the sun changes oft for a blessing or a curse, and the course of the path of the moon is light to the righteous and darkness to the sinners in the name of the Lord. Who made a separation between the light and the darkness, and divided the spirits of men, and strengthened the spirits of the righteous in the name of His righteousness.

44 For no angel hinders and no power is able to hinder; for He appoints a judge for them all and He judges them all before Him.

45 Wisdom found no place where she might dwell, then a dwelling place was assigned her in the heavens.

46 Wisdom went forth to make her dwelling among the children of men and found no dwelling place.

47 Wisdom returned to her place and took her seat among the angels.

48 And unrighteousness went forth from her chambers: Whom she sought not she found and dwelt with them, as rain in a desert and dew on a thirsty land.

49 And I saw other lightnings and the stars of heaven, and I saw how He called them all by their names and they hearkened unto Him.

50 And I saw how they are weighed in a righteous balance according to their proportions of light: the width of their spaces and the day of their appearing, and how their revolution produces lightning: and their revolution according to the number of the angels, and they keep faith with each other.

51 And I asked the angel who went with me who showed me what was hidden: "What are these?"

52 And he said to me: "The Lord of Spirits hath showed thee their parabolic meaning: these are the names of the holy who dwell on the earth and believe in the name of the Lord of Spirits for ever and ever."

53 Also another phenomenon I saw in regard to the lightnings: how some of the stars arise and become lightnings and cannot part with their new form.

Chapter 2
The Second Parable

1 And this is the second Parable concerning those who deny the name of the dwelling of the holy ones and the Lord of Spirits.

2 And into the heaven they shall not ascend, and on the earth they shall not come. Such shall be the lot of the sinners who have denied the name of the Lord of Spirits. Who are thus preserved for the day of suffering and tribulation.

3 On that day Mine Elect One shall sit on the throne of glory and shall try their works, and their places of rest shall be innumerable. And their souls shall grow strong within them when they see Mine Elect Ones.

4 And those who have called upon My glorious name: Then will I cause Mine Elect One to dwell among them.

5 And I will transform the heaven and make it an eternal blessing and light and I will transform the earth and make it a blessing: and I will cause Mine Elect Ones to dwell upon it: But the sinners and evil doers shall not set foot thereon.

6 For I have provided and satisfied with peace My righteous ones and have caused them to dwell before Me: But for the sinners there is judgement impending with Me, so that I shall destroy them from the face of the earth.

7 And there I saw One who had a head of days, and His head was white like wool, and with Him was another being whose countenance had the appearance of a man, and his face was full of graciousness, like one of the holy angels.

8 And I asked the angel who went with me and showed me all the hidden things, concerning that Son of Man, who he was, and whence he was, and why he went with the Head of Days.

9 And he answered and said unto me: "This is the Son of Man who hath righteousness. With whom dwelleth righteousness, and who reveals all the treasures of that which is hidden. Because the Lord of Spirits hath chosen him, and whose lot hath preeminence before the Lord of Spirits in uprightness for ever.

10 And this Son of Man whom thou hast seen shall raise up the kings and the mighty from their seats and shall loosen the reins of the strong, and break the

teeth of the sinners. Because they do not extol and praise Him, Nor humbly acknowledge whence the kingdom was bestowed upon them.

11 And he shall put down the countenance of the strong, and shall fill them with shame. Darkness shall be their dwelling and worms shall be their bed. They shall have no hope of rising from their beds because they do not extol the name of the Lord of Spirits.

12 These are they who judge the stars of heaven, tread upon the earth, and dwell upon it.

13 All their deeds manifest unrighteousness and their power rests upon their riches.

14 Their faith is in the gods which they have made with their hands and they deny the name of the Lord of Spirits.

15 They persecute the houses of His congregations and the faithful who hang upon the name of the Lord of Spirits.

16 And in those days shall have ascended the prayer of the righteous and the blood of the righteous from the earth before the Lord of Spirits.

17 In those days the holy ones who dwell above in the heavens shall unite with one voice and supplicate and pray and praise, give thanks and bless the name of the Lord of Spirits on behalf of the blood of the righteous which has been shed.

18 And that the prayer of the righteous may not be in vain before the Lord of Spirits, that judgement may be done unto them and that they may not have to suffer for ever."

19 In those days I saw the Head of Days when He seated himself upon the throne of His glory, and the books of the living were opened before Him, and all His host which is in heaven above and His counselors stood before Him.

20 And the hearts of the holy were filled with joy because the number of the righteous had been offered, and the prayer of the righteous had been heard, and the blood of the righteous been required before the Lord of Spirits.

21 And in that place I saw the fountain of righteousness, which was inexhaustible; and around it were many fountains of wisdom. All the thirsty drank of them and were filled with wisdom and their dwellings were with the righteous and holy and elect.

22 And at that hour that Son of Man was named in the presence of the Lord of Spirits, and His name before the Head of Days.

23 Yea, before the sun and the signs were created, before the stars of the heaven were made, His name was named before the Lord of Spirits.

24 "He shall be a staff to the righteous whereon to stay themselves and not fall and he shall be the light of the Gentiles, and the hope of those who are troubled of heart.

25 All who dwell on earth shall fall down and worship before Him, and will praise and bless and celebrate with song the Lord of Spirits.

26 And for this reason hath He been chosen and hidden before Him, before the creation of the world and for evermore.

27 And the wisdom of the Lord of Spirits hath revealed Him to the holy and righteous for He hath preserved the lot of the righteous because they have hated and despised this world of unrighteousness and have hated all its works and ways in the name of the Lord of Spirits: For in his name they are saved and according to His good pleasure hath it been in regard to their life.

28 In these days downcast in countenance shall the kings of the earth have become and the strong who possess the land because of the works of their hands. For on the day of their anguish and affliction they shall not save themselves and I will give them over into the hands of Mine Elect.

29 As straw in the fire so shall they burn before the face of the holy: As lead in the water shall they sink before the face of the righteous and no trace of them shall any more be found.

30 And on the day of their affliction there shall be rest on the earth, and before them they shall fall and not rise again. There shall be no one to take them with his hands and raise them for they have denied the Lord of Spirits and His Anointed One. The name of the Lord of Spirits be blessed.

31 For wisdom is poured out like water, and glory faileth not before Him for evermore.

32 For He is mighty in all the secrets of righteousness and unrighteousness shall disappear as a shadow and have no continuance. Because the Elect One standeth

before the Lord of Spirits and His glory is for ever and ever and His might unto all generations.

33 And in Him dwells the spirit of wisdom, and the spirit which gives insight, and the spirit of understanding and of might, and the spirit of those who have fallen asleep in righteousness.

34 And He shall judge the secret things and none shall be able to utter a lying word before Him for He is the Elect One before the Lord of Spirits according to His good pleasure.

35 In those days a change shall take place for the Holy and Elect, and the Light of Days shall abide upon them and glory and honor shall turn to the holy.

36 On the day of affliction on which evil shall have been treasured up against the sinners. And the righteous shall be victorious in the name of the Lord of Spirits and He will cause the others to witness that they may repent and forgo the works of their hands.

37 They shall have no honor through the name of the Lord of Spirits yet through His name shall they be saved, and the Lord of Spirits will have compassion on them for His compassion is great.

38 And He is righteous also in His judgement and in the presence of His glory unrighteousness also shall not maintain itself: At His judgement the unrepentant shall perish before Him.

39 And from henceforth, I will have no mercy on them." saith the Lord of Spirits.

40 In those days shall the earth also give back that which has been entrusted to it. Sheol also shall give back that which it has received, and hell shall give back that which it owes.

41 For in those days the Elect One shall arise and He shall choose the righteous and holy from among them.

42 For the day has drawn nigh that they should be saved.

43 And the Elect One shall in those days sit on My throne and His mouth shall pour forth all the secrets of wisdom and counsel for the Lord of Spirits hath given to Him and hath glorified Him.

44 In those days shall the mountains leap like rams and the hills also shall skip like lambs satisfied with milk, and the faces of the angels in heaven shall be lighted up with joy.

45 And the earth shall rejoice and the righteous shall dwell upon it and the Elect shall walk thereon.

46 And after those days in that place where I had seen all the visions of that which is hidden, for I had been carried off in a whirlwind and they had borne me towards the west.

47 There mine eyes saw all the secret things of heaven that shall be, a mountain of iron, and a mountain of copper, and a mountain of silver, and a mountain of gold, and a mountain of soft metal, and a mountain of lead.

48 And I asked the angel who went with me, saying, "What things are these which I have seen in secret?"

49 And he said unto me: "All these things which thou hast seen shall serve the dominion of His Anointed that He may be potent and mighty on the earth."

50 And that angel of peace answered, saying unto me: "Wait a little, and there shall be revealed unto thee all the secret things which surround the Lord of Spirits.

51 And these mountains which thine eyes have seen, the mountain of iron, and the mountain of copper, and the mountain of silver, and the mountain of gold, and the mountain of soft metal, and the mountain of lead.

52 All these shall be in the presence of the Elect One as wax before the fire, and like the water which streams down from above and they shall become powerless before his feet.

53 And it shall come to pass in those days that none shall be saved either by gold or by silver and none be able to escape.

54 And there shall be no iron for war. Nor shall one clothe oneself with a breastplate. Bronze shall be of no service, and tin shall not be esteemed, and lead shall not be desired.

55 And all these things shall be destroyed from the surface of the earth."

56 And I looked and turned to another part of the earth, and saw there a deep valley with burning fire. And they brought the kings and the mighty, and began to cast them into this deep valley.

57 And there mine eyes saw how they made these their instruments, iron chains of immeasurable weight.

58 And I asked the angel of peace who went with me, saying: "For whom are these chains being prepared?"

59 And he said unto me: "These are being prepared for the hosts of Azazel, so that they may take them and cast them into the abyss of complete condemnation, and they shall cover their jaws with rough stones as the Lord of Spirits commanded."

60 And Michael, and Gabriel, and Raphael, and Phanuel shall take hold of them on that great day, and cast them on that day into the burning furnace, that the Lord of Spirits may take vengeance on them for their unrighteousness in becoming subject to Satan and leading astray those who dwell on the earth.

61 And in those days shall punishment come from the Lord of Spirits, and He will open all the chambers of waters which are above the heavens, and of the fountains which are beneath the earth.

62 And all the waters shall be joined with the waters: that which is above the heavens is the masculine, and the water which is beneath the earth is the feminine.

63 And they shall destroy all who dwell on the earth and those who dwell under the ends of the heaven. And when they have recognized their unrighteousness which they have wrought on the earth, then by these shall they perish.

64 And after that, the Head of Days repented and said: "In vain have I destroyed all who dwell on the earth."

65 And He sware by His great name: "Henceforth I will not do so to all who dwell on the earth and I will set a sign in the heaven and this shall be a pledge of good faith between Me and them for ever. So long as heaven is above the earth and this is in accordance with My command.

66 When I have desired to take hold of them by the hand of the angels on the day of tribulation and pain because of this, I will cause My chastisement and My wrath to abide upon them." saith God, the Lord of Spirits.

67 Ye mighty kings who dwell on the earth, ye shall have to behold Mine Elect One. How He sits on the throne of glory and judges Azazel and all his associates, and all his hosts in the name of the Lord of Spirits.

68 And I saw there the hosts of the angels of punishment going and they held scourges and chains of iron and bronze.

69 And I asked the angel of peace who went with me, saying: "To whom are these who hold the scourges going?"

70 And he said unto me: "To their elect and beloved ones, that they may be cast into the chasm of the abyss of the valley."

71 And then that valley shall be filled with their elect and beloved, and the days of their lives shall be at an end, and the days of their leading astray shall not thenceforward be reckoned.

72 And in those days the angels shall return and hurl themselves to the east upon the Parthians and Medes.

73 They shall stir up the kings, so that a spirit of unrest shall come upon them and they shall rouse them from their thrones that they may break forth as lions from their lairs and as hungry wolves among their flocks.

74 And they shall go up and tread under foot the land of His elect ones but the city of the righteous shall be a hindrance to their horses.

75 And they shall begin to fight among themselves and their right hand shall be strong against themselves.

76 And a man shall not know his brother nor a son his father or his mother till there be no number of the corpses through their slaughter and their punishment be not in vain.

77 In those days Sheol shall open its jaws and they shall be swallowed up therein. Their destruction shall be at an end. Sheol shall devour the sinners in the presence of the elect."

78 And it came to pass after this that I saw another host of wagons, and men riding thereon, and coming on the winds from the east, and from the west to the south.

79 And the noise of their wagons was heard, and when this turmoil took place the holy ones from heaven remarked it, and the pillars of the earth were moved from their place, and the sound thereof was heard from the one end of heaven to the other, in one day.

80 And they shall all fall down and worship the Lord of Spirits. And this is the end of the second Parable.

Chapter 3
The Third Parable

1 And I began to speak the third Parable concerning the righteous and elect.

2 Blessed are ye, ye righteous and Elect for glorious shall be your lot.

3 And the righteous shall be in the light of the sun and the elect in the light of eternal life.

4 The days of their life shall be unending and the days of the holy without number.

5 And they shall seek the light and find righteousness with the Lord of Spirits.

6 There shall be peace to the righteous in the name of the Eternal Lord.

7 And after this it shall be said to the holy in heaven that they should seek out the secrets of righteousness, the heritage of faith.

8 For it has become bright as the sun upon earth and the darkness is past.

9 And there shall be a light that never ends and to a limit of days they shall not come.

10 For the darkness shall first have been destroyed and the light of uprightness established for ever before the Lord of Spirits.

11 In those days mine eyes saw the secrets of the lightnings, and of the lights, and the judgements they execute, and they lighten for a blessing or a curse as the Lord of Spirits willeth.

12 And there I saw the secrets of the thunder, and how when it resounds above in the heaven, the sound thereof is heard.

13 And He caused me to see the judgements executed on the earth, whether they be for well being and blessing, or for a curse according to the word of the Lord of Spirits.

14 And after that, all the secrets of the lights and lightnings were shown to me, and they lighten for blessing and for satisfying.

15 In the year 500, in the seventh month, on the fourteenth day of the month in the life of Enoch.

16 In that parable I saw how a mighty quaking made the heaven of heavens to quake, and the host of the Most High, and the angels, a thousand thousands and ten thousand times ten thousand were disquieted with a great disquiet.

17 And the Head of Days sat on the throne of His glory, and the angels and the righteous stood around Him.

18 And a great trembling seized me, and fear took hold of me, and my loins gave way, and dissolved were my reins, and I fell upon my face.

19 And Michael sent another angel from among the holy ones and he raised me up, and when he had raised me up my spirit returned; for I had not been able to endure the look of this host, and the commotion and the quaking of the heaven.

20 And Michael said unto me: Why art thou disquieted with such a vision? Until this day lasted the day of His mercy; and He hath been merciful and long suffering towards those who dwell on the earth.

21 And when the day, and the power, and the punishment, and the judgement come, which the Lord of Spirits hath prepared for those who worship not the righteous law, and for those who deny the righteous judgement, and for those who take His name in vain, that day is prepared, for the elect a covenant, but for sinners an inquisition.

22 When the punishment of the Lord of Spirits shall rest upon them, it shall rest in order that the punishment of the Lord of Spirits may not come in vain, and it shall slay the children with their mothers and the children with their fathers.

23 Afterwards the judgement shall take place according to His mercy and His patience."

24 And on that day were two monsters parted, a female monster named Leviathan, to dwell in the abysses of the ocean over the fountains of the waters.

25 But the male is named Behemoth, who occupied with his breast a waste wilderness named Duidain, on the east of the garden where the elect and righteous dwell, where my grandfather was taken up, the seventh from Adam, the first man whom the Lord of Spirits created.

26 And I besought the other angel that he should show me the might of those monsters, how they were parted on one day and cast, the one into the abysses of the sea and the other unto the dry land of the wilderness.

27 And he said to me: "Thou son of man, herein thou dost seek to know what is hidden."

28 And the other angel who went with me and showed me what was hidden told me what is first and last in the heaven in the height, and beneath the earth in the depth, and at the ends of the heaven, and on the foundation of the heaven.

29 And the chambers of the winds, and how the winds are divided, and how they are weighed, and how the portals of the winds are reckoned, each according to the power of the wind, and the power of the lights of the moon, and according to the power that is fitting: and the divisions of the stars according to their names and how all the divisions are divided.

30 And the thunders according to the places where they fall, and all the divisions that are made among the lightnings that it may lighten, and their host that they may at once obey.

31 For the thunder has places of rest assigned to it while it is waiting for its peal; and the thunder and lightning are inseparable, and although not one and undivided, they both go together through the spirit and separate not.

32 For when the lightning lightens, the thunder utters its voice, and the spirit enforces a pause during the peal, and divides equally between them; for the treasury of their peals is like the sand, and each one of them as it peals is held in with a bridle, and turned back by the power of the spirit, and pushed forward according to the many quarters of the earth.

33 And the spirit of the sea is masculine and strong, and according to the might of his strength he draws it back with a rein, and in like manner it is driven forward and disperses amid all the mountains of the earth.

34 And the spirit of the hoarfrost is his own angel, and the spirit of the hail is a good angel.

35 And the spirit of the snow has forsaken his chambers on account of his strength; there is a special spirit therein, and that which ascends from it is like smoke, and its name is Frost.

36 And the spirit of the mist is not united with them in their chambers, but it has a special chamber; for its course is glorious both in light and in darkness, and in winter and in summer, and in its chamber is an angel.

37 And the spirit of the dew has its dwelling at the ends of the heaven, and is connected with the chambers of the rain, and its course is in winter and summer: and its clouds and the clouds of the mist are connected, and the one gives to the other.

38 And when the spirit of the rain goes forth from its chamber, the angels come and open the chamber and lead it out, and when it is diffused over the whole earth it unites with the water on the earth. And whensoever it unites with the water on the earth.

39 For the waters are for those who dwell on the earth; for they are nourishment for the earth from the Most High who is in heaven: therefore there is a measure for the rain, and the angels take it in charge.

40 And these things I saw towards the Garden of the Righteous.

41 And the angel of peace who was with me said to me: "These two monsters, prepared conformably to the greatness of God, shall feed."

42 And I saw in those days how long cords were given to those angels, and they took to themselves wings and flew, and they went towards the north.

43 And I asked the angel, saying unto him: "Why have those angels taken these cords and gone off?"

44 And he said unto me: "They have gone to measure."

45 And the angel who went with me said unto me: "These shall bring the measures of the righteous and the ropes of the righteous to the righteous. That they may stay themselves on the name of the Lord of Spirits for ever and ever.

46 The elect shall begin to dwell with the elect, and those are the measures which shall be given to faith and which shall strengthen righteousness.

47 And these measures shall reveal all the secrets of the depths of the earth. And those who have been destroyed by the desert, and those who have been devoured by the beasts, and those who have been devoured by the fish of the sea. That they may return and stay themselves on the day of the Elect One; for none shall be destroyed before the Lord of Spirits, and none can be destroyed."

48 And all who dwell above in the heaven received a command and power and one voice and one light like unto fire.

49 And that One with their first words they blessed and extolled and lauded with wisdom.

50 And they were wise in utterance and in the spirit of life.

51 And the Lord of Spirits placed the Elect one on the throne of glory. And he shall judge all the works of the holy above in the heaven, and in the balance shall their deeds be weighed.

52 And thus the Lord commanded the kings and the mighty and the exalted, and those who dwell on the earth, and said: "Open your eyes and lift up your horns if ye are able to recognize the Elect One."

53 And the Lord of Spirits seated him on the throne of His glory and the spirit of righteousness was poured out upon Him.

54 And the word of his mouth slays all the sinners, and all the unrighteous are destroyed from before his face.

55 And there shall stand up in that day all the kings and the mighty, and the exalted and those who hold the earth, and they shall see and recognize how He sits on the throne of His glory.

56 And righteousness is judged before him and no lying word is spoken before him.

57 Then shall pain come upon them as on a woman in travail when her child enters the mouth of the womb and she has pain in bringing forth.

58 And one portion of them shall look on the other and they shall be terrified, and they shall be downcast of countenance, and pain shall seize them when they see that Son of Man sitting on the throne of his glory.

59 And the kings and the mighty and all who possess the earth shall bless and glorify and extol him who rules over all, who was hidden.

60 For from the beginning the Son of Man was hidden and the Most High preserved Him in the presence of His might, and revealed Him to the elect.

61 And the congregation of the elect and holy shall be sown and all the elect shall stand before him on that day.

62 And all the kings and the mighty and the exalted and those who rule the earth shall fall down before Him on their faces and worship and set their hope upon that Son of Man, and petition him and supplicate for mercy at his hands.

63 Nevertheless that Lord of Spirits will so press them that they shall hastily go forth from His presence, and their faces shall be filled with shame, and the darkness grow deeper on their faces.

64 And He will deliver them to the angels for punishment to execute vengeance on them because they have oppressed His children and His elect.

65 And they shall be a spectacle for the righteous and for His elect: They shall rejoice over them because the wrath of the Lord of Spirits resteth upon them and His sword is drunk with their blood.

66 And the righteous and elect shall be saved on that day, and they shall never thenceforward see the face of the sinners and unrighteous.

67 And the Lord of Spirits will abide over them, and with that Son of Man shall they eat and lie down and rise up for ever and ever.

68 And the righteous and elect shall have risen from the earth and ceased to be of downcast countenance.

69 And they shall have been clothed with garments of glory and these shall be the garments of life from the Lord of Spirits: And your garments shall not grow old. Nor your glory pass away before the Lord of Spirits.

70 In those days shall the mighty and the kings who possess the earth implore to grant them a little respite from His angels of punishment to whom they were delivered, that they might fall down and worship before the Lord of Spirits and confess their sins before Him.

71 And they shall bless and glorify the Lord of Spirits, and say: "Blessed is the Lord of Spirits and the Lord of kings, and the Lord of the mighty and the Lord of the rich, and the Lord of glory and the Lord of wisdom, and splendid in every secret thing is Thy power from generation to generation, and Thy glory for ever and ever.

72 Deep are all Thy secrets and innumerable, and Thy righteousness is beyond reckoning. We have now learnt that we should glorify and bless the Lord of kings and Him who is king over all kings."

73 And they shall say: "Would that we had rest to glorify and give thanks and confess our faith before His glory! And now we long for a little rest but find it not. We follow hard upon and obtain not, and light has vanished from before us, and darkness is our dwelling place for ever and ever.

74 For we have not believed before Him nor glorified the name of the Lord of Spirits but our hope was in the sceptre of our kingdom, and in our own glory.

75 And in the day of our suffering and tribulation He saves us not and we find no respite for confession that our Lord is true in all His works, and in His judgements and His justice, and His judgements have no respect of persons.

76 And we pass away from before His face on account of our works and all our sins are reckoned up in righteousness."

77 Now they shall say unto themselves: "Our souls are full of unrighteous gain, but it does not prevent us from descending from the midst thereof into the burden of Sheol."

78 And after that their faces shall be filled with darkness and shame before that Son of Man, and they shall be driven from his presence, and the sword shall abide before his face in their midst.

79 Thus spake the Lord of Spirits: "This is the ordinance and judgement with respect to the mighty and the kings and the exalted and those who possess the earth before the Lord of Spirits."

80 And other forms I saw hidden in that place. I heard the voice of the angel saying: "These are the angels who descended to the earth, and revealed what was hidden to the children of men and seduced the children of men into committing sin."

Book 3
The Book of Noah

Chapter 1
Birth of Noah

1 And after some days my son Methuselah took a wife for his son Lamech, and she became pregnant by him and bore a son.

2 And his body was white as snow and red as the blooming of a rose, and the hair of his head and his long locks were white as wool, and his eyes beautiful. And when he opened his eyes, he lighted up the whole house like the sun, and the whole house was very bright.

3 And thereupon he arose in the hands of the midwife, opened his mouth, and conversed with the Lord of righteousness.

4 And his father Lamech was afraid of him and fled, and came to his father Methuselah.

5 And he said unto him: "I have begotten a strange son, diverse from and unlike man, and resembling the sons of the God of heaven; and his nature is different and he is not like us, and his eyes are as the rays of the sun, and his countenance is glorious.

6 And it seems to me that he is not sprung from me but from the angels, and I fear that in his days a wonder may be wrought on the earth. And now, my father, I am here to petition thee and implore thee that thou mayest go to Enoch, our father, and learn from him the truth, for his dwelling place is amongst the angels."

7 And when Methuselah heard the words of his son, he came to me to the ends of the earth; for he had heard that I was there, and he cried aloud, and I heard his voice and I came to him.

8 And I said unto him: "Behold, here am I, my son, wherefore hast thou come to me?"

9 And he answered and said: "Because of a great cause of anxiety have I come to thee, and because of a disturbing vision have I approached.

10 And now, my father, hear me: unto Lamech my son there hath been born a son, the like of whom there is none, and his nature is not like mans nature, and the color of his body is whiter than snow and redder than the bloom of a rose, and the

hair of his head is whiter than white wool, and his eyes are like the rays of the sun, and he opened his eyes and thereupon lighted up the whole house.

11 And he arose in the hands of the midwife, and opened his mouth and blessed the Lord of heaven.

12 And his father Lamech became afraid and fled to me, and did not believe that he was sprung from him, but that he was in the likeness of the angels of heaven; and behold I have come to thee that thou mayest make known to me the truth."

13 And I, Enoch, answered and said unto him: "The Lord will do a new thing on the earth, and this I have already seen in a vision, and make known to thee that in the generation of my father Jared some of the angels of heaven transgressed the word of the Lord.

14 And behold they commit sin and transgress the law, and have united themselves with women and commit sin with them, and have married some of them, and have begot children by them.

15 And they shall produce on the earth giants not according to the spirit, but according to the flesh, and there shall be a great punishment on the earth, and the earth shall be cleansed from all impurity.

16 Yea, there shall come a great destruction over the whole earth, and there shall be a deluge and a great destruction for one year.

17 And this son who has been born unto you shall be left on the earth, and his three children shall be saved with him: when all mankind that are on the earth shall die he and his sons shall be saved.

18 And now make known to thy son Lamech that he who has been born is in truth his son, and call his name Noah; for he shall be left to you, and he and his sons shall be saved from the destruction which shall come upon the earth on account of all the sin and all the unrighteousness, which shall be consummated on the earth in his days.

19 And after that there shall be still more unrighteousness than that which was first consummated on the earth; for I know the mysteries of the holy ones; for He, the Lord, has showed me and informed me, and I have read in the heavenly tablets.

20 And I saw written on them that generation upon generation shall transgress, till a generation of righteousness arises, and transgression is destroyed and sin passes away from the earth, and all manner of good comes upon it.

21 And now, my son, go and make known to thy son Lamech that this son, which has been born, is in truth his son, and that is no lie."

22 And when Methuselah had heard the words of his father Enoch for he had shown to him everything in secret he returned and showed to him and called the name of that son Noah; for he will comfort the earth after all the destruction.

Chapter 2
Calling Enoch

1 And in those days Noah saw the earth that it had sunk down and its destruction was nigh.

2 And he arose from thence and went to the ends of the earth, and cried aloud to his grandfather Enoch.

3 Noah said three times with an embittered voice: "Hear me, hear me, hear me."

4 And I said unto him: "Tell me what it is that is falling out on the earth that the earth is in such evil plight and shaken, lest perchance I shall perish with it?"

5 And thereupon there was a great commotion , on the earth, and a voice was heard from heaven, and I fell on my face.

6 And Enoch my grandfather came and stood by me, and said unto me: "Why hast thou cried unto me with a bitter cry and weeping?

7 A command has gone forth from the presence of the Lord concerning those who dwell on the earth that their ruin is accomplished because they have learnt all the secrets of the angels, and all the violence of the Satans, and all their powers, the most secret ones.

8 And all the power of those who practice sorcery, and the power of witchcraft, and the power of those who make molten images. For the whole earth: And how silver is produced from the dust of the earth, and how soft metal originates in the earth. For lead and tin are not produced from the earth like the first: it is a fountain that produces them, and an angel stands therein, and that angel is preeminent."

9 And after that my grandfather Enoch took hold of me by my hand and raised me up, and said unto me: "Go, for I have asked the Lord of Spirits as touching this commotion on the earth.

10 And He said unto me: "Because of their unrighteousness their judgement has been determined upon and shall not be withheld by Me for ever. Because of the sorceries which they have searched out and learnt, the earth and those who dwell upon it shall be destroyed."

11 And these, they have no place of repentance for ever, because they have shown them what was hidden, and they are the damned: but as for thee, my son, the Lord of Spirits knows that thou art pure, and guiltless of this reproach concerning the secrets.

12 And He has destined thy name to be among the holy and will preserve thee amongst those who dwell on the earth. And has destined thy righteous seed both for kingship and for great honors, and from thy seed shall proceed a fountain of the righteous and holy without number for ever."

13 And after that he showed me the angels of punishment who are prepared to come and let loose all the powers of the waters which are beneath in the earth in order to bring judgement and destruction on all who dwell on the earth.

14 And the Lord of Spirits gave commandment to the angels who were going forth that they should not cause the waters to rise but should hold them in check; for those angels were over the powers of the waters.

15 And I went away from the presence of Enoch.

Chapter 3
Judgement of Angels

1 And in those days the word of God came unto me, and He said unto me: "Noah, thy lot has come up before Me, a lot without blame, a lot of love and uprightness.

2 And now the angels are working, and when they have completed their task I will place My hand upon it and preserve it, and there shall come forth from it the seed of life, and a change shall set in so that the earth will not remain without inhabitant.

3 And I will make fast thy seed before me for ever and ever, and I will spread abroad those who dwell with thee: it shall not be unfruitful on the face of the earth, but it shall be blessed and multiply on the earth in the name of the Lord."

4 And He will imprison those angels, who have shown unrighteousness in that burning valley which my grandfather Enoch had formerly shown to me in the west among the mountains of gold and silver and iron and soft metal and tin.

5 And I saw that valley in which there was a great convulsion and a convulsion of the waters.

6 And when all this took place, from that fiery molten metal and from the convulsion thereof in that place, there was produced a smell of sulphur, and it was connected with those waters, and that valley of the angels who had led astray burned beneath that land.

7 And through its valleys proceed streams of fire where these angels are punished who had led astray those who dwell upon the earth.

8 But those waters shall in those days serve for the kings and the mighty and the exalted, and those who dwell on the earth, for the healing of the body, but for the punishment of the spirit; now their spirit is full of lust, that they may be punished in their body.

9 For they have denied the Lord of Spirits and see their punishment daily, and yet believe not in His name.

10 And in proportion as the burning of their bodies becomes severe a corresponding change shall take place in their spirit for ever and ever; for before the Lord of Spirits none shall utter an idle word.

11 For the judgement shall come upon them because they believe in the lust of their body and deny the Spirit of the Lord.

12 And those same waters will undergo a change in those days; for when those angels are punished in these waters, these water springs shall change their temperature, and when the angels ascend, this water of the springs shall change and become cold.

13 And I heard Michael answering and saying: "This judgement wherewith the angels are judged is a testimony for the kings and the mighty who possess the earth.

14 Because these waters of judgement minister to the healing of the body of the kings and the lust of their body; therefore they will not see and will not believe that those waters will change and become a fire which burns for ever."

Chapter 4
Secrets of the Parables

1 And after that my grandfather Enoch gave me the teaching of all the secrets in the book in the Parables which had been given to him, and he put them together for me in the words of the book of the Parables.

2 And on that day Michael answered Raphael and said: "The power of the spirit transports and makes me to tremble because of the severity of the judgement of the secrets, the judgement of the angels: who can endure the severe judgement which has been executed, and before which they melt away?"

3 And Michael answered again, and said to Raphael: "Who is he whose heart is not softened concerning it, and whose reins are not troubled by this word of judgement that has gone forth upon them because of those who have thus led them out?"

4 And it came to pass when he stood before the Lord of Spirits, Michael said thus to Raphael: "I will not take their part under the eye of the Lord; for the Lord of Spirits has been angry with them because they do as if they were the Lord. Therefore all that is hidden shall come upon them for ever and ever; for neither angel nor man shall have his portion, but alone they have received their judgement for ever and ever."

5 And after this judgement they shall terrify and make them to tremble because they have shown this to those who dwell on the earth.

6 And behold the names of those angels: the first of them is Samjaza, the second Artaqifa, and the third Armen, the fourth Kokabel, the fifth Turael, the sixth Rumjal, the seventh Danjal, the eighth Neqael, the ninth Baraqel, the tenth Azazel, the eleventh Armaros, the twelfth Batarjal, the thirteenth Busasejal, the fourteenth Hananel, the fifteenth Turel, and the sixteenth Simapesiel, the seventeenth Jetrel, the eighteenth Tumael, the nineteenth Turel, the twentieth Rumael, the twenty first Azazel.

7 And these are the chiefs of their angels and their names, and their chief ones over hundreds and over fifties and over tens.

8 The name of the first Jeqon: that is, the one who led astray the sons of God, and brought them down to the earth, and led them astray through the daughters of men.

9 And the second was named Asbeel: he imparted to the holy sons of God evil counsel, and led them astray so that they defiled their bodies with the daughters of men.

10 And the third was named Gadreel: he it is who showed the children of men all the blows of death, and he led astray Eve, and showed the shield and the coat of mail, and the sword for battle, and all the weapons of death to the children of men. And from his hand they have proceeded against those who dwell on the earth from that day and for evermore.

11 And the fourth was named Penemue: he taught the children of men the bitter and the sweet, and he taught them all the secrets of their wisdom. And he instructed mankind in writing with ink and paper, and thereby many sinned from eternity to eternity and until this day. For men were not created for such a purpose, to give confirmation to their good faith with pen and ink. For men were created exactly like the angels, to the intent that they should continue pure and righteous, and death, which destroys everything, could not have taken hold of them but through this their knowledge they are perishing, and through this power it is consuming men.

12 And the fifth was named Kasdeja: this is he who showed the children of men all the wicked smithings of spirits and demons, and the smitings of the embryo in the womb, that it may pass away, and the bites of the serpent, and the smitings which befall through the noontide heat the son of the serpent named Tabaet.

13 And this is the task of Kasbeel, the chief of the oath which he showed to the holy ones when he dwelt high above in glory, and its name is Biqa.

14 This angel requested Michael to show him the hidden name, that he might enunciate it in the oath, so that those might quake before that name and oath who revealed all that was in secret to the children of men.

15 And this is the power of this oath, for it is powerful and strong, and he placed this oath Akae in the hand of Michael.

16 These are the secrets of this oath and they are strong through his oath: The heaven was suspended before the world was created, and for ever.

17 And through it the earth was founded upon the water and from the secret recesses of the mountains come beautiful waters from the creation of the world and unto eternity.

18 And through that oath the sea was created and as its foundation He set for it the sand against the time of anger, and it dare not pass beyond it from the creation of the world unto eternity.

19 And through that oath are the depths made fast and abide and stir not from their place from eternity to eternity.

20 And through that oath the sun and moon complete their course and deviate not from their ordinance from eternity to eternity.

21 And through that oath the stars complete their course and He calls them by their names, and they answer Him from eternity to eternity.

22 And this oath is mighty over them and through it their paths are preserved and their course is not destroyed.

23 And there was great joy amongst them, and they blessed and glorified and extolled because the name of that Son of Man had been revealed unto them.

24 And he sat on the throne of His glory and the sum of judgement was given unto the Son of Man, and He caused the sinners to pass away and be destroyed from off the face of the earth, and those who have led the world astray.

25 With chains shall they be bound and in their assemblage place of destruction shall they be imprisoned, and all their works vanish from the face of the earth.

26 And from henceforth there shall be nothing corruptible; For that Son of Man has appeared and has seated himself on the throne of His glory.

27 All evil shall pass away before His face and the word of that Son of Man shall go forth and be strong before the Lord of Spirits.

Book 4
The Kingdom of Heaven

Chapter 1
Enoch is Taken

1 And it came to pass after this that his name during his lifetime was raised aloft to that Son of Man and to the Lord of Spirits from amongst those who dwell on the earth.

2 And he was raised aloft on the chariots of the spirit and his name vanished among them.

3 And from that day I was no longer numbered amongst them and He set me between the two winds, between the North and the West, where the angels took the cords to measure for me the place for the elect and righteous.

4 And there I saw the first fathers and the righteous who from the beginning dwell in that place.

5 And it came to pass after this that my spirit was translated and it ascended into the heavens I saw the holy sons of God.

6 They were stepping on flames of fire: Their garments were white and their faces shone like snow.

7 And I saw two streams of fire and the light of that fire shone like hyacinth, and I fell on my face before the Lord of Spirits.

8 And the angel Michael seized me by my right hand and lifted me up and led me forth into all the secrets, and he showed me all the secrets of righteousness.

9 And he showed me all the secrets of the ends of the heaven, and all the chambers of all the stars, and all the luminaries, Whence they proceed before the face of the holy ones.

10 And he translated my spirit into the heaven of heavens and I saw there as it were a structure built of crystals and between those crystals tongues of living fire.

11 And my spirit saw the girdle which girt that house of fire and on its four sides were streams full of living fire, and they girt that house.

12 And round about were Seraphin, Cherubic, and Ophannin: And these are they who sleep not and guard the throne of His glory.

13 And I saw angels who could not be counted. A thousand thousands and ten thousand times ten thousand encircling that house.

14 And Michael, and Raphael, and Gabriel, and Phanuel, and the holy angels who are above the heavens go in and out of that house.

15 And they came forth from that house, and Michael and Gabriel, Raphael, and Phanuel, and many holy angels without number.

16 And with them the Head of Days, His head white and pure as wool, and His raiment indescribable.

17 And I fell on my face and my whole body became relaxed, and my spirit was transfigured; and I cried with a loud voice with the spirit of power and blessed and glorified and extolled.

18 And these blessings which went forth out of my mouth were well pleasing before that Head of Days.

19 And that Head of Days came with Michael and Gabriel, Raphael, and Phanuel, thousands and ten thousands of angels without number.

20 And He came to me and greeted me with His voice, and said unto me: "This is the Son of Man who is born unto righteousness, and righteousness abides over Him, and the righteousness of the Head of Days forsakes Him not."

21 And he said unto me: "He proclaims unto thee peace in the name of the world to come; for from hence has proceeded peace since the creation of the world, and so shall it be unto thee for ever and for ever and ever.

22 And all shall walk in his ways since righteousness never forsaketh Him.

23 With Him will be their dwelling places, and with Him their heritage, and they shall not be separated from Him for ever and ever and ever.

24 And so there shall be length of days with that Son of Man and the righteous shall have peace and an upright way in the name of the Lord of Spirits for ever and ever.

Chapter 2
The Luminaries

1 The book of the courses of the luminaries of the heaven, the relations of each, according to their classes, their dominion and their seasons, according to their names and places of origin, and according to their months, which Uriel, the holy angel, who was with me, who is their guide showed me.

2 And he showed me all their laws exactly as they are, and how it is with regard to all the years of the world and unto eternity, till the new creation is accomplished which dureth till eternity.

3 And this is the first law of the luminaries: the luminary the sun has its rising in the eastern portals of the heaven, and its setting in the western portals of the heaven.

4 And I saw six portals in which the sun rises, and six portals in which the sun sets and the moon rises and sets in these portals, and the leaders of the stars and those whom they lead: six in the east and six in the west, and all following each other in accurately corresponding order: also many windows to the right and left of these portals.

5 And first there goes forth the great luminary, named the sun, and his circumference is like the circumference of the heaven, and he is quite filled with illuminating and heating fire.

6 The chariot on which he ascends, the wind drives, and the sun goes down from the heaven and returns through the north in order to reach the east, and is so guided that he comes to the appropriate portal and shines in the face of the heaven.

7 In this way he rises in the first month in the great portal, which is the fourth. And in that fourth portal from which the sun rises in the first month are twelve window openings, from which proceed a flame when they are opened in their season.

8 When the sun rises in the heaven, he comes forth through that fourth portal thirty mornings in succession, and sets accurately in the fourth portal in the west of the heaven.

9 And during this period the day becomes daily longer and the night nightly shorter to the thirtieth morning.

10 On that day the day is longer than the night by a ninth part, and the day amounts exactly to ten parts and the night to eight parts.

11 And the sun rises from that fourth portal, and sets in the fourth and returns to the fifth portal of the east thirty mornings and rises from it and sets in the fifth portal.

12 And then the day becomes longer by two parts and amounts to eleven parts, and the night becomes shorter and amounts to seven parts.

13 And it returns to the east and enters into the sixth portal, and rises and sets in the sixth portal one and thirty mornings on account of its sign.

14 On that day the day becomes longer than the night, and the day becomes double the night, and the day becomes twelve parts, and the night is shortened and becomes six parts.

15 And the sun mounts up to make the day shorter and the night longer, and the sun returns to the east and enters into the sixth portal and rises from it and sets thirty mornings.

16 And when thirty mornings are accomplished, the day decreases by exactly one part, and becomes eleven parts, and the night seven.

17 And the sun goes forth from that sixth portal in the west, and goes to the east and rises in the fifth portal for thirty mornings, and sets in the west again in the fifth western portal.

18 On that day the day decreases by two parts, and amounts to ten parts and the night to eight parts.

19 And the sun goes forth from that fifth portal and sets in the fifth portal of the west, and rises in the fourth portal for one and thirty mornings on account of its sign, and sets in the west.

20 On that day the day is equalized with the night, and the night amounts to nine parts and the day to nine parts.

21 And the sun rises from that portal and sets in the west, and returns to the east and rises thirty mornings in the third portal and sets in the west in the third portal.

22 And on that day the night becomes longer than the day, and night becomes longer than night, and day shorter than day till the thirtieth morning, and the night amounts exactly to ten parts and the day to eight parts.

23 And the sun rises from that third portal and sets in the third portal in the west and returns to the east and for thirty mornings rises in the second portal in the east, and in like manner sets in the second portal in the west of the heaven.

24 And on that day the night amounts to eleven parts and the day to seven parts.

25 And the sun rises on that day from that second portal and sets in the west in the second portal, and returns to the east into the first portal for one and thirty mornings, and sets in the first portal in the west of the heaven.

26 And on that day the night becomes longer and amounts to the double of the day: and the night amounts exactly to twelve parts and the day to six.

27 And the sun has traversed the divisions of his orbit and turns again on those divisions of his orbit, and enters that portal thirty mornings and sets also in the west opposite to it.

28 And on that night has the night decreased in length by a ninth part, and the night has become eleven parts and the day seven parts.

29 And the sun has returned and entered into the second portal in the east, and returns on those his divisions of his orbit for thirty mornings, rising and setting.

30 And on that day the night decreases in length, and the night amounts to ten parts and the day to eight.

31 And on that day the sun rises from that portal, and sets in the west, and returns to the east, and rises in the third portal for one and thirty mornings, and sets in the west of the heaven.

32 On that day the night decreases and amounts to nine parts, and the day to nine parts, and the night is equal to the day and the year is exactly as to its days three hundred and sixty four.

33 And the length of the day and of the night, and the shortness of the day and of the night arise through the course of the sun these distinctions are made.

34 So it comes that its course becomes daily longer, and its course nightly shorter.

35 And this is the law and the course of the sun, and his return as often as he returns sixty times and rises for ever and ever.

36 And that which rises is the great luminary, and is so named according to its appearance, according as the Lord commanded.

37 As he rises, so he sets and decreases not, and rests not, but runs day and night, and his light is sevenfold brighter than that of the moon; but as regards size they are both equal.

38 And after this law I saw another law dealing with the smaller luminary, which is named the Moon.

39 And her circumference is like the circumference of the heaven, and her chariot in which she rides is driven by the wind, and light is given to her in measure.

40 And her rising and setting change every month and her days are like the days of the sun, and when her light is uniform it amounts to the seventh part of the light of the sun.

41 And thus she rises. And her first phase in the east comes forth on the thirtieth morning: and on that day she becomes visible and constitutes for you the first phase of the moon on the thirtieth day together with the sun in the portal where the sun rises.

42 And the one half of her goes forth by a seventh part, and her whole circumference is empty, without light, with the exception of one seventh part of it, the fourteenth part of her light.

43 And when she receives one seventh part of the half of her light, her light amounts to one seventh part and the half thereof.

44 And she sets with the sun, and when the sun rises the moon rises with him and receives the half of one part of light, and in that night in the beginning of her morning in the commencement of the lunar day the moon sets with the sun, and is invisible that night with the fourteen parts and the half of one of them.

45 And she rises on that day with exactly a seventh part, and comes forth and recedes from the rising of the sun, and in her remaining days she becomes bright in the thirteen parts.

46 And I saw another course, a law for her, how according to that law she performs her monthly revolution.

47 And all these Uriel, the holy angel who is the leader of them all showed to me, and their positions, and I wrote down their positions as he showed them to me, and I wrote down their months as they were, and the appearance of their lights till fifteen days were accomplished.

48 In single seventh parts she accomplishes all her light in the east, and in single seventh parts accomplishes all her darkness in the west.

49 And in certain months she alters her settings, and in certain months she pursues her own peculiar course.

50 In two months the moon sets with the sun: in those two middle portals the third and the fourth. She goes forth for seven days, and turns about and returns again through the portal where the sun rises, and accomplishes all her light and she recedes from the sun, and in eight days enters the sixth portal from which the sun goes forth.

51 And when the sun goes forth from the fourth portal she goes forth seven days, until she goes forth from the fifth and turns back again in seven days into the fourth portal and accomplishes all her light: and she recedes and enters into the first portal in eight days.

52 And she returns again in seven days into the fourth portal from which the sun goes forth.

53 Thus I saw their position, how the moons rose and the sun set in those days.

54 And if five years are added together the sun has an overplus of thirty days, and all the days which accrue to it for one of those five years, when they are full, amount to 364 days.

55 And the overplus of the sun and of the stars amounts to six days: in 5 years 6 days every year come to 30 days: and the moon falls behind the sun and stars to the number of 30 days.

56 And the sun and the stars bring in all the years exactly, so that they do not advance or delay their position by a single day unto eternity; but complete the years with perfect justice in 364 days.

57 In 3 years there are 1,092 days, and in 5 years 1,820 days, so that in 8 years there are 2,912 days.

58 For the moon alone the days amount in 3 years to 1,062 days, and in 5 years she falls 50 days behind to the sum there is 5 to be added 62 days.

59 And in 5 years there are 1,770 days, so that for the moon the days 6 in 8 years amount to 21,832 days.

60 For in 8 years she falls behind to the amount of 80 days, all the 17 days she falls behind in 8 years are 80.

61 And the year is accurately completed in conformity with their world stations and the stations of the sun, which rise from the portals through which it rises and sets 30 days.

62 And the leaders of the heads of the thousands, who are placed over the whole creation and over all the stars, have also to do with the four intercalary days, being inseparable from their office, according to the reckoning of the year, and these render service on the four days which are not reckoned in the reckoning of the year.

63 And owing to them men go wrong therein, for those luminaries truly render service on the world stations, one in the first portal, one in the third portal of the heaven, one in the fourth portal, and one in the sixth portal, and the exactness of the year is accomplished through its separate three hundred and sixty four stations.

64 For the signs and the times and the years and the days the angel Uriel showed to me, whom the Lord of glory hath set for ever over all the luminaries of the heaven, in the heaven and in the world that they should rule on the face of the heaven and be seen on the earth and be leaders for the day and the night and all the ministering creatures which make their revolution in all the chariots of the heaven.

65 In like manner twelve doors Uriel showed me open in the circumference of the suns chariot in the heaven, through which the rays of the sun break forth: and from them is warmth diffused over the earth, when they are opened at their appointed seasons.

66 And for the winds and the spirit of the dew when they are opened, standing open in the heavens at the ends.

67 As for the twelve portals in the heaven at the ends of the earth, out of which go forth the sun, moon, and stars, and all the works of heaven in the east and in the west.

68 There are many windows open to the left and right of them, and one window at its season produces warmth, corresponding to those doors from which the stars come forth according as He has commanded them and wherein they set corresponding to their number.

69 And I saw chariots in the heaven, running in the world, above those portals in which revolve the stars that never set.

70 And one is larger than all the rest and it is that that makes its course through the entire world.

71 And at the ends of the earth I saw twelve portals open to all the quarters from which the winds go forth and blow over the earth.

72 Three of them are open on the face of the heavens, and three in the west, and three on the right of the heaven, and three on the left.

73 And the three first are those of the east, and three are of the north, and three after those on the left of the south, and three of the west.

74 Through four of these come winds of blessing and prosperity and from those eight come hurtful winds: when they are sent, they bring destruction on all the earth and on the water upon it, and on all who dwell thereon, and on everything which is in the water and on the land.

75 And the first wind from those portals, called the east wind, comes forth through the first portal which is in the east, inclining towards the south: from it come forth desolation, drought, heat, and destruction.

76 And through the second portal in the middle comes what is fitting, and from it there come rain and fruitfulness and prosperity and dew; and through the third portal which lies toward the north come cold and drought.

77 And after these come forth the south winds through three portals: through the first portal of them inclining to the east comes forth a hot wind.

78 And through the middle portal next to it there come forth fragrant smells, and dew and rain, and prosperity and health.

79 And through the third portal lying to the west come forth dew and rain, locusts and desolation.

80 And after these the north winds: from the seventh portal in the east come dew and rain, locusts and desolation.

81 And from the middle portal come in a direct direction health and rain and dew and prosperity; and through the third portal in the west come cloud and hoarfrost, and snow and rain, and dew and locusts.

82 And after these four are the west winds: through the first portal adjoining the north come forth dew and hoarfrost, and cold and snow and frost.

83 And from the middle portal come forth dew and rain, and prosperity and blessing; and through the last portal which adjoins the south come forth drought and desolation, and burning and destruction.

84 And the twelve portals of the four quarters of the heaven are therewith completed and all their laws and all their plagues and all their benefactions have I shown to thee, my son Methuselah.

85 And the first quarter is called the east because it is the first. And the second, the south, because the Most High will descend there, yea, there in quite a special sense will He who is blessed for ever descend.

86 And the west quarter is named the diminished because there all the luminaries of the heaven wane and go down.

87 And the fourth quarter named the north, is divided into three parts: the first of them is for the dwelling of men: and the second contains seas of water, and the abysses and forests and rivers, and darkness and clouds; and the third part contains the garden of righteousness.

88 I saw seven high mountains, higher than all the mountains which are on the earth and thence comes forth hoarfrost, and days, seasons, and years pass away.

89 I saw seven rivers on the earth larger than all the rivers: one of them coming from the west pours its waters into the Great Sea.

90 And these two come from the north to the sea and pour their waters into the Erythraean Sea in the east.

91 And the remaining, four come forth on the side of the north to their own sea, two of them to the Erythraean Sea, and two into the Great Sea and discharge themselves there and some say, into the desert.

92 Seven great islands I saw in the sea and in the mainland: two in the mainland and five in the Great Sea.

93 And the names of the sun are the following: the first Orjares, and the second Tomas.

94 And the moon has four names: the first name is Asonja, the second Ebla, the third Benase, and the fourth Erae.

95 These are the two great luminaries: their circumference is like the circumference of the heaven, and the size of the circumference of both is alike.

96 In the circumference of the sun there are seven portions of light which are added to it more than to the moon, and in definite measures it is s transferred till the seventh portion of the sun is exhausted.

97 And they set and enter the portals of the west, and make their revolution by the north, and come forth through the eastern portals on the face of the heaven.

98 And when the moon rises one fourteenth part appears in the heaven: the light becomes full in her : on the fourteenth day she accomplishes her light.

99 And fifteen parts of light are transferred to her till the fifteenth day her light is accomplished, according to the sign of the year, and she becomes fifteen parts, and the moon grows by fourteenth parts.

100 And in her waning decreases on the first day to fourteen parts of her light, on the second to thirteen parts of light, on the third to twelve, on the fourth to eleven, on the fifth to ten, on the sixth to nine, on the seventh to eight, on the eighth to seven, on the ninth to six, on the tenth to five, on the eleventh to four, on the twelfth to three, on the thirteenth to two, on the fourteenth to the half of a seventh, and all her remaining light disappears wholly on the fifteenth.

101 And in certain months the month has twenty nine days and once twenty eight.

102 And Uriel showed me another law: when light is transferred to the moon, and on which side it is transferred to her by the sun.

103 During all the period during which the moon is growing in her light, she is transferring it to herself when opposite to the sun during fourteen daysher light is accomplished in the heaven, and when she is illumined throughout, her light is accomplished full in the heaven.

104 And on the first day she is called the new moon, for on that day the light rises upon her. She becomes full moon exactly on the day when the sun sets in the west, and from the east she rises at night, and the moon shines the whole night through till the sun rises over against her and the moon is seen over against the sun.

105 On the side whence the light of the moon comes forth, there again she wanes till all the light vanishes and all the days of the month are at an end and her circumference is empty, void of light.

106 And three months she makes of thirty days, and at her time she makes three months of twenty nine days each, in which she accomplishes her waning in the first period of time, and in the first portal for one hundred and seventy seven days.

107 And in the time of her going out she appears for three months thirty days each, and for three months she appears twenty nine each.

108 At night she appears like a man for twenty days each time, and by day she appears like the heaven, and there is nothing else in her save her light.

109 And now, my son, I have shown thee everything, and the law of all the stars of the heaven is completed.

110 And he showed me all the laws of these for every day, and for every season of bearing rule, and for every year, and for its going forth, and for the order prescribed to it every month and every week: And the waning of the moon which takes place in the sixth portal: for in this 4 sixth portal her light is accomplished.

111 And after that there is the beginning of the waning which takes place in the first portal in its season, till one hundred and seventy seven days are accomplished: reckoned according to weeks, twenty five and two days.

112 She falls behind the sun and the order of the stars exactly five days in the course of one period, and when this place which thou seest has been traversed.

113 Such is the picture and sketch of every luminary which Uriel the archangel, who is their leader, showed unto me.

Chapter 3
Heavenly Tablets

1 And in those days the angel Uriel answered and said to me: "Behold, I have shown thee everything Enoch and I have revealed everything to thee that thou shouldst see this sun and this moon, and the leaders of the stars of the heaven and all those who turn them, their tasks and times and departures.

2 And in the days of the sinners the years shall be shortened and their seed shall be tardy on their lands and fields.

3 And all things on the earth shall alter and shall not appear in their time: The rain shall be kept back and the heaven shall withhold it.

4 And in those times the fruits of the earth shall be backward and shall not grow in their time, and the fruits of the trees shall be withheld in their time.

5 And the moon shall alter her order and not appear at her time.

6 And in those days the sun shall be seen and he shall journey in the evening on the extremity of the great chariot in the west and shall shine more brightly than accords with the order of light.

7 And many chiefs of the stars shall transgress the order and these shall alter their orbits and tasks and not appear at the seasons prescribed to them.

8 And the whole order of the stars shall be concealed from the sinners and the thoughts of those on the earth shall err concerning them. And they shall be altered from all their ways. Yea, they shall err and take them to be gods.

9 And evil shall be multiplied upon them, and punishment shall come upon them so as to destroy all."

10 And He said unto me: "Observe, Enoch, these heavenly tablets and read what is written thereon, and mark every individual fact."

11 And I observed the heavenly tablets, and read everything which was written and understood everything, and read the book of all the deeds of mankind, and of all the children of flesh that shall be upon the earth to the remotest generations.

12 And forthwith I blessed the great Lord the King of glory for ever, in that He has made all the works of the world.

13 And I extolled the Lord because of His patience and blessed Him because of the children of men.

14 And after that I said: "Blessed is the man who dies in righteousness and goodness concerning whom there is no book of unrighteousness written, and against whom no day of judgement shall be found."

15 And those seven holy ones brought me and placed me on the earth before the door of my house, and said to me: "Declare everything to thy son Methuselah, and show to all thy children that no flesh is righteous in the sight of the Lord, for He is their Creator.

16 One year we will leave thee with thy son, till thou givest thy commands, that thou mayest teach thy children and record for them, and testify to all thy children; and in the second year they shall take thee from their midst.

17 Let thy heart be strong, for the good shall announce righteousness to the good; The righteous with the righteous shall rejoice and shall offer congratulation to one another.

18 But the sinners shall die with the sinners and the apostate go down with the apostate.

19 And those who practice righteousness shall die on account of the deeds of men and be taken away on account of the doings of the godless.

20 And in those days they ceased to speak to me, and I came to my people, blessing the Lord of the world.

Chapter 4
One Year to Record

1 And now, my son Methuselah, all these things I am recounting to thee and writing down for thee! and I have revealed to thee everything, and given thee books concerning all these: so preserve, my son Methuselah, the books from thy fathers hand, and see that thou deliver them to the generations of the world.

2 I have given wisdom to thee and to thy children and thy children that shall be to thee, that they may give it to their children for generations, this wisdom that passeth their thought.

3 And those who understand it shall not sleep but shall listen with the ear that they may learn this wisdom and it shall please those that eat thereof better than good food.

4 Blessed are all the righteous, blessed are all those who walk in the way of righteousness and sin not as the sinners.

5 In the reckoning of all their days in which the sun traverses the heaven, entering into and departing from the portals for thirty days with the heads of thousands of the order of the stars, together with the four which are intercalated which divide the four portions of the year, which lead them and enter with them four days.

6 Owing to them men shall be at fault and not reckon them in the whole reckoning of the year: yea, men shall be at fault, and not recognize them accurately.

7 For they belong to the reckoning of the year and are truly recorded for ever, one in the first portal and one in the third, and one in the fourth and one in the sixth, and the year is completed in three hundred and sixty four days.

8 And the account thereof is accurate and the recorded reckoning thereof exact; for the luminaries, and months and festivals, and years and days, has Uriel shown and revealed to me, to whom the Lord of the whole creation of the world hath subjected the host of heaven.

9 And he has power over night and day in the heaven to cause the light to give light to men, sun, moon, and stars, and all the powers of the heaven which revolve in their circular chariots.

10 And these are the orders of the stars, which set in their places, and in their seasons and festivals and months.

11 And these are the names of those who lead them, who watch that they enter at their times, in their orders, in their seasons, in their months, in their periods of dominion, and in their positions.

12 Their four leaders who divide the four parts of the year enter first; and after them the twelve leaders of the orders who divide the months; and for the three hundred and sixty there are heads over thousands who divide the days; and for the four intercalary days there are the leaders which sunder the four parts of the year.

13 And these heads over thousands are intercalated between leader and leader, each behind a station, but their leaders make the division.

14 And these are the names of the leaders who divide the four parts of the year which are ordained: Milkiel, Helemmelek, and Melejal, and Narel.

15 And the names of those who lead them: Adnarel, and Ijasusael, and Elomeel - these three follow the leaders of the orders, and there is one that follows the three leaders of the orders which follow those leaders of stations that divide the four parts of the year.

16 In the beginning of the year Melkejal rises first and rules, who is named Tamaini and sun, and all the days of his dominion whilst he bears rule are ninety one days.

17 And these are the signs of the days which are to be seen on earth in the days of his dominion: sweat, and heat, and calms; and all the trees bear fruit, and leaves are produced on all the trees, and the harvest of wheat, and the rose flowers, and all the flowers which come forth in the field, but the trees of the winter season become withered.

18 And these are the names of the leaders which are under them: Berkael, Zelebsel, and another who is added a head of a thousand, called Hilujaseph: and the days of the dominion of this are at an end.

19 The next leader after him is Helemmelek, whom one names the shining sun, and all the days of his light are ninety one days. And these are the signs of days on the earth: glowing heat and dryness, and the trees ripen their fruits and produce all their fruits ripe and ready, and the sheep pair and become pregnant,

and all the fruits of the earth are gathered in, and everything that is in the fields, and the winepress: these things take place in the days of his dominion.

20 These are the names, and the orders, and the leaders of those heads of thousands: Gidaljal, Keel, and Heel, and the name of the head of a thousand which is added to them, Asfael: and the days of his dominion are at an end.

Chapter 5
Visions

1 And now, my son Methuselah, I will show thee all my visions which I have seen, recounting them before thee.

2 Two visions I saw before I took a wife, and the one was quite unlike the other. The first when I was learning to write: the second before I took thy mother I saw a terrible vision.

3 And regarding them I prayed to the Lord. I had laid me down in the house of my grandfather Mahalaleel I saw in a vision how the heaven collapsed and was borne off and fell to the earth.

4 And when it fell to the earth I saw how the earth was swallowed up in a great abyss, and mountains were suspended on mountains, and hills sank down on hills, and high trees were rent from their stems and hurled down and sunk in the abyss.

5 And thereupon a word fell into my mouth and I lifted up to cry aloud, and said: "The earth is destroyed!"

6 And my grandfather Mahalaleel waked me as I lay near him, and said unto me: "Why dost thou cry so my son, and why dost thou make such lamentation?"

7 And I recounted to him the whole vision which I had seen, and he said unto me: "A terrible thing hast thou seen, my son, and of grave moment is thy dream vision as to the secrets if all the sin of the earth: it must sink into the abyss and be destroyed with a great destruction.

8 And now, my son, arise and make petition to the Lord of glory, since thou art a believer that a remnant may remain on the earth, and that He may not destroy the whole earth. My son, from heaven all this will come upon the earth, and upon the earth there will be great destruction."

9 After that I arose and prayed and implored and besought, and wrote down my prayer for the generations of the world, and I will show everything to thee, my son Methuselah.

10 And when I had gone forth below and seen the heaven and the sun rising in the east, and the moon setting in the west, and a few stars, and the whole earth, and everything as He had known it in the beginning then I blessed the Lord of

judgement and extolled Him because He had made the sun to go forth from the windows of the east, and He ascended and rose on the face of the heaven, and set out and kept traversing the path shown unto Him.

11 And I lifted up my hands in righteousness and blessed the Holy and Great One and spake with the breath of my mouth, and with the tongue of flesh which God has made for the children of the flesh of men that they should speak therewith, and He gave them breath and a tongue and a mouth that they should speak therewith:

12 "Blessed be Thou, O Lord, King, Great and mighty in Thy greatness, Lord of the whole creation of the heaven, King of kings and God of the whole world.

13 And Thy power and kingship and greatness abide for ever and ever, and throughout all generations Thy dominion; and all the heavens are Thy throne for ever, and the whole earth Thy footstool for ever and ever.

14 For Thou hast made and Thou rulest all things and nothing is too hard for Thee.

15 Wisdom departs not from the place of Thy throne nor turns away from Thy presence.

16 And Thou knowest and seest and hearest everything and there is nothing hidden from Thee for Thou seest everything.

17 And now the angels of Thy heavens are guilty of trespass and upon the flesh of men abideth Thy wrath until the great day of judgement.

18 And now, O God and Lord and Great King, I implore and beseech Thee to fulfil my prayer to leave me a posterity on earth and not destroy all the flesh of man and make the earth without inhabitant so that there should be an eternal destruction.

19 And now, my Lord, destroy from the earth the flesh which has aroused Thy wrath but the flesh of righteousness and uprightness establish as a plant of the eternal seed and hide not Thy face from the prayer of Thy servant, O Lord."

20 And after this I saw another dream, and I will show the whole dream to thee, my son.

21 And Enoch lifted up and spake to his son Methuselah: "To thee, my son, will I speak: hear my words incline thine ear to the dream vision of thy father.

22 Before I took thy mother Edna, I saw in a vision on my bed, and behold a bull came forth from the earth, and that bull was white; and after it came forth a heifer, and along with this came forth two bulls, one of them black and the other red.

23 And that black bull gored the red one and pursued him over the earth, and thereupon I could no longer see that red bull.

24 But that black bull grew and that heifer went with him, and I saw that many oxen proceeded from him which resembled and followed him.

25 And that cow, that first one, went from the presence of that first bull in order to seek that red one, but found him not, and lamented with a great lamentation over him and sought him.

26 And I looked till that first bull came to her and quieted her, and from that time onward she cried no more.

27 And after that she bore another white bull, and after him she bore many bulls and black cows.

28 And I saw in my sleep that white bull likewise grow and become a great white bull, and from him proceeded many white bulls, and they resembled him. And they began to beget many white bulls, which resembled them, one following the other, many.

29 And again I saw with mine eyes as I slept, and I saw the heaven above, and behold a star fell from heaven, and it arose and eat and pastured amongst those oxen.

30 And after that I saw the large and the black oxen, and behold they all changed their stalls and pastures and their cattle, and began to live with each other.

31 And again I saw in the vision, and looked towards the heaven, and behold I saw many stars descend and cast themselves down from heaven to that first star, and they became bulls amongst those cattle and pastured with them amongst them.

32 And I looked at them and saw, and behold they all let out their privy members, like horses, and began to cover the cows of the oxen, and they all became pregnant and bare elephants, camels, and asses.

33 And all the oxen feared them and were affrighted at them, and began to bite with their teeth and to devour, and to gore with their horns.

34 And they began, moreover, to devour those oxen; and behold all the children of the earth began to tremble and quake before them and to flee from them.

35 And again I saw how they began to gore each other and to devour each other, and the earth began to cry aloud.

36 And I raised mine eyes again to heaven, and I saw in the vision, and behold there came forth from heaven beings who were like white men: and four went forth from that place and three with them.

37 And those three that had last come forth grasped me by my hand and took me up away from the generations of the earth, and raised me up to a lofty place, and showed me a tower raised high above the earth and all the hills were lower.

38 And one said unto me: "Remain here till thou seest everything that befalls those elephants, camels, and asses, and the stars and the oxen, and all of them."

39 And I saw one of those four who had come forth first, and he seized that first star which had fallen from the heaven, and bound it hand and foot and cast it into an abyss.

40 Now that abyss was narrow and deep, and horrible and dark.

41 And one of them drew a sword, and gave it to those elephants and camels and asses: then they began to smite each other, and the whole earth quaked because of them.

42 And as I was beholding in the vision, lo, one of those four who had come forth stoned them from heaven, and gathered and took all the great stars whose privy members were like those of horses and bound them all hand and foot, and cast them in an abyss of the earth.

43 And one of those four went to that white bull and instructed him in a secret without his being terrified: he was born a bull and became a man, and built for himself a great vessel and dwelt thereon; and three bulls dwelt with him in that vessel and they were covered in.

44 And again I raised mine eyes towards heaven and saw a lofty roof, with seven water torrents thereon and those torrents flowed with much water into an enclosure.

45 And I saw again, and behold fountains were opened on the surface of that great enclosure, and that water began to swell and rise upon the surface and I saw that enclosure till all its surface was covered with water.

46 And the water, the darkness, and mist increased upon it; and as I looked at the height of that water, that water had risen above the height of that enclosure, and was streaming over that enclosure, and it stood upon the earth.

47 And all the cattle of that enclosure were gathered together until I saw how they sank and were swallowed up and perished in that water.

48 But that vessel floated on the water, while all the oxen and elephants and camels and asses sank to the bottom with all the animals, so that I could no longer see them, and they were not able to escape, perished and sank into the depths.

49 And again I saw in the vision till those water torrents were removed from that high roof, and the chasms of the earth were leveled up and other abysses were opened.

50 Then the water began to run down into these, till the earth became visible; but that vessel settled on the earth, and the darkness retired and light appeared.

51 But that white bull which had become a man came out of that vessel, and the three bulls with him, and one of those three was white like that bull, and one of them was red as blood, and one black: and that white bull departed from them.

52 And they began to bring forth beasts of the field and birds, so that there arose different genera: lions, tigers, wolves, dogs, hyenas, wild boars, foxes, squirrels, swine, falcons, vultures, kites, eagles, and ravens; and among them was born a white bull.

53 And they began to bite one another; but that white bull which was born amongst them begat a wild ass and a white bull with it, and the wild asses multiplied. But that bull which was born from him begat a black wild boar and a white sheep; and the former begat many boars, but that sheep begat twelve sheep.

54 And when those twelve sheep had grown, they gave up one of them to the asses, and those asses again gave up that sheep to the wolves, and that sheep grew up among the wolves.

55 And the Lord brought the eleven sheep to live with it and to pasture with it among the wolves: and they multiplied and became many flocks of sheep.

56 And the wolves began to fear them, and they oppressed them until they destroyed - cry aloud on account of their little ones, and to complain unto their Lord.

57 And a sheep which had been saved from the wolves fled and escaped to the wild asses; and I saw the sheep how they lamented and cried, and besought their Lord with all their might, till that Lord of the sheep descended at the voice of the sheep from a lofty abode, and came to them and pastured them.

58 And He called that sheep which had escaped the wolves, and spake with it concerning the wolves that it should admonish them not to touch the sheep.

59 And the sheep went to the wolves according to the word of the Lord, and another sheep met it and went with it, and the two went and entered together into the assembly of those wolves, and spake with them and admonished them not to touch the sheep from henceforth.

60 And thereupon I saw the wolves, and how they oppressed the sheep exceedingly with all their power; and the sheep cried aloud.

61 And the Lord came to the sheep and they began to smite those wolves and the wolves began to make lamentation; but the sheep became quiet and forthwith ceased to cry out.

62 And I saw the sheep till they departed from amongst the wolves; but the eyes of the wolves were blinded, and those wolves departed in pursuit of the sheep with all their power.

63 And the Lord of the sheep went with them, as their leader, and all His sheep followed Him: and his face was dazzling and glorious and terrible to behold.

64 But the wolves began to pursue those sheep till they reached a sea of water. And that sea was divided, and the water stood on this side and on that before their face, and their Lord led them and placed Himself between them and the wolves.

65 And as those wolves did not yet see the sheep, they proceeded into the midst of that sea, and the wolves followed the sheep, and those wolves ran after them into that sea.

66 And when they saw the Lord of the sheep, they turned to flee before His face, but that sea gathered itself together, and became as it had been created, and the water swelled and rose till it covered those wolves.

67 And I saw till all the wolves who pursued those sheep perished and were drowned.

68 But the sheep escaped from that water and went forth into a wilderness, where there was no water and no grass; and they began to open their eyes and to see; and I saw the Lord of the sheep pasturing them and giving them water and grass, and that sheep going and leading them.

69 And that sheep ascended to the summit of that lofty rock, and the Lord of the sheep sent it to them.

70 And after that I saw the Lord of the sheep who stood before them, and His appearance was great and terrible and majestic, and all those sheep saw Him and were afraid before His face.

71 And they all feared and trembled because of Him, and they cried to that sheep with them which was amongst them: "We are not able to stand before our Lord or to behold Him."

72 And that sheep which led them again ascended to the summit of that rock, but the sheep began to be blinded and to wander from the way which he had showed them, but that sheep wot not thereof.

73 And the Lord of the sheep was wrathful exceedingly against them, and that sheep discovered it, and went down from the summit of the rock, and came to the sheep, and found the greatest part of them blinded and fallen away.

74 And when they saw it they feared and trembled at its presence, and desired to return to their folds.

75 And that sheep took other sheep with it, and came to those sheep which had fallen away, and began to slay them; and the sheep feared its presence, and thus that sheep brought back those sheep that had fallen away, and they returned to their folds.

76 And I saw in this vision till that sheep became a man and built a house for the Lord of the sheep, and placed all the sheep in that house.

77 And I saw till this sheep which had met that sheep which led them fell asleep: and I saw till all the great sheep perished and little ones arose in their place, and they came to a pasture, and approached a stream of water.

78 Then that sheep, their leader which had become a man, withdrew from them and fell asleep, and all the sheep sought it and cried over it with a great crying.

79 And I saw till they left off crying for that sheep and crossed that stream of water, and there arose the two sheep as leaders in the place of those which had led them and fallen asleep.

80 And I saw till the sheep came to a goodly place, and a pleasant and glorious land, and I saw till those sheep were satisfied; and that house stood amongst them in the pleasant land.

81 And sometimes their eyes were opened, and sometimes blinded, till another sheep arose and led them and brought them all back, and their eyes were opened.

82 And the dogs and the foxes and the wild boars began to devour those sheep till the Lord of the sheep raised up another sheep a ram from their midst, which led them. And that ram began to butt on either side those dogs, foxes, and wild boars till he had destroyed them all.

83 And that sheep whose eyes were opened saw that ram, which was amongst the sheep, till it forsook its glory and began to butt those sheep and trampled upon them, and behaved itself unseemly.

84 And the Lord of the sheep sent the lamb to another lamb and raised it to being a ram and leader of the sheep instead of that ram which had forsaken its glory.

85 And it went to it and spake to it alone, and raised it to being a ram, and made it the prince and leader of the sheep; but during all these things those dogs oppressed the sheep.

86 And the first ram pursued that second ram, and that second ram arose and fled before it; and I saw till those dogs pulled down the first ram.

87 And that second ram arose and led the little sheep. And those sheep grew and multiplied; but all the dogs, and foxes, and wild boars feared and fled before it, and that ram butted and killed the wild beasts, and those wild beasts had no longer any power among the 49sheep and robbed them no more of ought.

88 And that ram begat many sheep and fell asleep; and a little sheep became ram in its stead, and became prince and leader of those sheep and that house became great and broad, and it was built for those sheep.

89 A tower lofty and great was built on the house for the Lord of the sheep, and that house was low, but the tower was elevated and lofty, and the Lord of the sheep stood on that tower and they offered a full table before Him.

90 And again I saw those sheep that they again erred and went many ways, and forsook that their house, and the Lord of the sheep called some from amongst the sheep and sent them to the sheep, but the sheep began to slay them.

91 And one of them was saved and was not slain, and it sped away and cried aloud over the sheep; and they sought to slay it, but the Lord of the sheep saved it from the sheep, and brought it up to me, and caused it to dwell there.

92 And many other sheep He sent to those sheep to testify unto them and lament over them.

93 And after that I saw that when they forsook the house of the Lord and His tower they fell away entirely, and their eyes were blinded; and I saw the Lord of the sheep how He wrought much slaughter amongst them in their herds until those sheep invited that slaughter and betrayed His place.

94 And He gave them over into the hands of the lions and tigers, and wolves and hyenas, and into the hand of the foxes, and to all the wild beasts, and those wild beasts began to tear in pieces those sheep.

95 And I saw that He forsook that their house and their tower and gave them all into the hand of the lions, to tear and devour them, into the hand of all the wild beasts.

96 And I began to cry aloud with all my power, and to appeal to the Lord of the sheep, and to represent to Him in regard to the sheep that they were devoured by all the wild beasts.

97 But He remained unmoved, though He saw it, and rejoiced that they were devoured and swallowed and robbed, and left them to be devoured in the hand of all the beasts.

98 And He called seventy shepherds, and cast those sheep to them that they might pasture them, and He spake to the shepherds and their companions: "Let each individual of you pasture the sheep henceforward, and everything that I shall command you that do ye. And I will deliver them over unto you duly numbered, and tell you which of them are to be destroyed and them destroy ye."

99 And He gave over unto them those sheep.

100 And He called another and spake unto him: "Observe and mark everything that the shepherds will do to those sheep; for they will destroy more of them than I have commanded them. And every excess and the destruction which will be wrought through the shepherds, record how many they destroy according to my command, and how many according to their own caprice: record against every individual shepherd all the destruction he effects. And read out before me by number how many they destroy, and how many they deliver over for destruction, that I may have this as a testimony against them, and know every deed of the shepherds, that I may comprehend and see what they do, whether or not they abide by my command which I have commanded them. But they shall not know it, and thou shalt not declare it to them, nor admonish them, but only record against each individual all the destruction which the shepherds effect each in his time and lay it all before me."

101 And I saw till those shepherds pastured in their season, and they began to slay and to destroy more than they were bidden, and they delivered those sheep into the hand of the lions.

102 And the lions and tigers eat and devoured the greater part of those sheep, and the wild boars eat along with them; and they burnt that tower and demolished that house.

103 And I became exceedingly sorrowful over that tower because that house of the sheep was demolished, and afterwards I was unable to see if those sheep entered that house.

104 And the shepherds and their associates delivered over those sheep to all the wild beasts, to devour them, and each one of them received in his time a definite number: it was written by the other in a book how many each one of them destroyed of them.

105 And each one slew and destroyed many more than was prescribed; and I began to weep and lament on account of those sheep.

106 And thus in the vision I saw that one who wrote, how he wrote down every one that was destroyed by those shepherds, day by day, and carried up and laid down and showed actually the whole book to the Lord of the sheep everything that they had done, and all that each one of them had made away with, and all that they had given over to destruction.

107 And the book was read before the Lord of the sheep, and He took the book from his hand and read it and sealed it and laid it down.

108 And forthwith I saw how the shepherds pastured for twelve hours, and behold three of those sheep turned back and came and entered and began to build up all that had fallen down of that house; but the wild boars tried to hinder them, but they were not able.

109 And they began again to build as before, and they reared up that tower, and it was named the high tower; and they began again to place a table before the tower, but all the bread on it was polluted and not pure.

110 And as touching all this the eyes of those sheep were blinded so that they saw not, and their shepherds likewise; and they delivered them in large numbers to their shepherds for destruction, and they trampled the sheep with their feet and devoured them.

111 And the Lord of the sheep remained unmoved till all the sheep were dispersed over the field and mingled with them and they did not save them out of the hand of the beasts.

112 And this one who wrote the book carried it up, and showed it and read it before the Lord of the sheep, and implored Him on their account, and besought Him on their account as he showed Him all the doings of the shepherds, and gave testimony before Him against all the shepherds.

113 And he took the actual book and laid it down beside Him and departed.

114 And I saw till that in this manner thirty five shepherds undertook the pasturing, and they severally completed their periods as did the first; and others receive them into their hands, to pasture them for their period, each shepherd in his own period.

115 And after that I saw in my vision all the birds of heaven coming, the eagles, the vultures, the kites, the ravens; but the eagles led all the birds; and they began to devour those sheep, and to pick out their eyes and to devour their flesh.

116 And the sheep cried out because their flesh was being devoured by the birds and as for me I looked and lamented in my sleep over that shepherd who pastured the sheep.

117 And I saw until those sheep were devoured by the dogs and eagles and kites, and they left neither flesh nor skin nor sinew remaining on them till only their bones stood there: and their bones too fell to the earth and the sheep became few.

118 And I saw until that twenty three had undertaken the pasturing and completed in their several periods fifty eight times.

119 But behold lambs were borne by those white sheep, and they began to open their eyes and to see, and to cry to the sheep.

120 Yea, they cried to them, but they did not hearken to what they said to them, but were exceedingly deaf, and their eyes were very exceedingly blinded.

121 And I saw in the vision how the ravens flew upon those lambs and took one of those lambs, and dashed the sheep in pieces and devoured them.

122 And I saw till horns grew upon those lambs, and the ravens cast down their horns; and I saw till there sprouted a great horn of one of those sheep, and their eyes were opened.

123 And it looked at them and their eyes opened, and it cried to the sheep, and the rams saw it and all ran to it.

124 And notwithstanding all this those eagles and vultures and ravens and kites still kept tearing the sheep and swooping down upon them and devouring them: still the sheep remained silent, but the rams lamented and cried out.

125 And those ravens fought and battled with it and sought to lay low its horn, but they had no power over it.

126 All the eagles and vultures and ravens and kites were gathered together and there came with them all the sheep of the field, yea, they all came together, and helped each other to break that horn of the ram.

127 And I saw till a great sword was given to the sheep, and the sheep proceeded against all the beasts of the field to slay them, and all the beasts and the birds of the heaven fled before their face.

128 And I saw that man, who wrote the book according to the command of the Lord, till he opened that book concerning the destruction which those twelve last shepherds had wrought, and showed that they had destroyed much more than their predecessors, before the Lord of the sheep.

129 And I saw till the Lord of the sheep came unto them and took in His hand the staff of His wrath, and smote the earth, and the earth clave asunder, and all the beasts and all the birds of the heaven fell from among those sheep, and were swallowed up in the earth and it covered them.

130 And I saw till a throne was erected in the pleasant land, and the Lord of the sheep sat Himself thereon, and the other took the sealed books and opened those books before the Lord of the sheep.

131 And the Lord called those men the seven first white ones, and commanded that they should bring before Him, beginning with the first star which led the way, all the stars whose privy members were like those of horses, and they brought them all before Him.

132 And He said to that man who wrote before Him, being one of those seven white ones, and said unto him: "Take those seventy shepherds to whom I delivered the sheep, and who taking them on their own authority slew more than I commanded them."

133 And behold they were all bound, I saw, and they all stood before Him.

134 And the judgement was held first over the stars, and they were judged and found guilty, and went to the place of condemnation, and they were cast into an abyss, full of fire and flaming, and full of pillars of fire.

135 And those seventy shepherds were judged and found guilty, and they were cast into that fiery abyss.

136 And I saw at that time how a like abyss was opened in the midst of the earth, full of fire, and they brought those blinded sheep, and they were all judged and found guilty and cast into this fiery abyss, and they burned; now this abyss was to the right of that house.

137 And I saw those sheep burning and their bones burning.

138 And I stood up to see till they folded up that old house; and carried off all the pillars, and all the beams and ornaments of the house were at the same time folded up with it, and they carried it off and laid it in a place in the south of the land.

139 And I saw till the Lord of the sheep brought a new house greater and loftier than that first, and set it up in the place of the first which had beer folded up: all its pillars were new, and its ornaments were new and larger than those of the first, the old one which He had taken away, and all the sheep were within it.

140 And I saw all the sheep which had been left, and all the beasts on the earth, and all the birds of the heaven, falling down and doing homage to those sheep and making petition to and obeying them in every thing.

141 And thereafter those three who were clothed in white and had seized me by my hand who had taken me up before, and the hand of that ram also seizing hold of me, they took me up and set me down in the midst of those sheep before the judgement took place.

142 And those sheep were all white, and their wool was abundant and clean.

143 And all that had been destroyed and dispersed, and all the beasts of the field, and all the birds of the heaven, assembled in that house, and the Lord of the sheep rejoiced with great joy because they were all good and had returned to His house.

144 And I saw till they laid down that sword, which had been given to the sheep, and they brought it back into the house, and it was sealed before the presence of the Lord, and all the sheep were invited into that house, but it held them not.

145 And the eyes of them all were opened, and they saw the good, and there was not one among them that did not see.

146 And I saw that that house was large and broad and very full.

147 And I saw that a white bull was born, with large horns and all the beasts of the field and all the birds of the air feared him and made petition to him all the time.

148 And I saw till all their generations were transformed, and they all became white bulls; and the first among them became a lamb, and that lamb became a great animal and had great black horns on its head; and the Lord of the sheep rejoiced over it and over all the oxen.

149 And I slept in their midst: and I awoke and saw everything.

150 This is the vision which I saw while I slept, and I awoke and blessed the Lord of righteousness and gave Him glory.

151 Then I wept with a great weeping and my tears stayed not till I could no longer endure it: when I saw, they flowed on account of what I had seen; for everything shall come and be fulfilled, and all the deeds of men in their order were shown to me.

152 On that night I remembered the first dream, and because of it I wept and was troubled because I had seen that vision.

Book 5
Epistle of Enoch

Chapter 1
The Guidance of Enoch

1 And now, my son Methuselah, call to me all thy brothers and gather together to me all the sons of thy mother; For the word calls me, and the spirit is poured out upon me that I may show you everything that shall befall you for ever.

2 And there upon Methuselah went and summoned to him all his brothers and assembled his relatives.

3 And he spake unto all the children of righteousness and said: "Hear, ye sons of Enoch, all the words of your father, and hearken aright to the voice of my mouth for I exhort you and say unto you, beloved:

4 Love uprightness and walk therein.
And draw not nigh to uprightness with a double heart,
And associate not with those of a double heart,
But walk in righteousness, my sons.

5 And it shall guide you on good paths, and righteousness shall be your companion.

6 For I know that violence must increase on the earth,
And a great chastisement be executed on the earth,
And all unrighteousness come to an end:
Yea, it shall be cut off from its roots,
And its whole structure be destroyed.

7 And unrighteousness shall again be consummated on the earth,
And all the deeds of unrighteousness and of violence,
And transgression shall prevail in a twofold degree.

8 And when sin and unrighteousness and blasphemy,
And violence in all kinds of deeds increase,
And apostasy and transgression and uncleanness increase,
A great chastisement shall come from heaven upon all these,
And the holy Lord will come forth with wrath and chastisement,
To execute judgement on earth.

9 In those days violence shall be cut off from its roots,
And the roots of unrighteousness together with deceit,
And they shall be destroyed from under heaven.

10 And all the idols of the heathen shall be abandoned,
And the temples burned with fire,
And they shall remove them from the whole earth,
And they shall be cast into the judgement of fire,
And shall perish in wrath and in grievous judgement for ever.

11 And the righteous shall arise from their sleep,
And wisdom shall arise and be given unto them.

12 And after that the roots of unrighteousness shall be cut off, and the sinners shall be destroyed by the sword and the blasphemers destroyed in every place, and those who plan violence and those who commit blasphemy shall perish by the sword.

13 And now I tell you, my sons, and show you the paths of righteousness and the paths of violence.

14 Yea, I will show them to you again that ye may know what will come to pass.

15 And now, listen to me, my sons,
And walk in the paths of righteousness,
And walk not in the paths of violence;
For all who walk in the paths of unrighteousness shall perish for ever."

Chapter 2
Wisdom of Enoch

1 The book written by Enoch. Enoch indeed wrote this complete doctrine of wisdom, praised of all men and a judge of all the earth for all my children who shall dwell on the earth. And for the future generations who shall observe uprightness and peace.

2 "Let not your spirit be troubled on account of the times; For the Holy and Great One has appointed days for all things.

3 And the righteous one shall arise from sleep, shall arise and walk in the paths of righteousness and all his path and conversation shall be in eternal goodness and grace.

4 He will be gracious to the righteous and give him eternal uprightness, and He will give him power so that he shall be with goodness and righteousness.

5 And he shall walk in eternal light.

6 And sin shall perish in darkness for ever and shall no more be seen from that day for evermore."

7 And after that Enoch both gave and began to recount from the books.

8 And Enoch said: "Concerning the children of righteousness and concerning the elect of the world, and concerning the plant of uprightness, I will speak these things.

9 Yea, I Enoch will declare unto you, my sons: According to that which appeared to me in the heavenly vision, and which I have known through the word of the holy angels, and have learnt from the heavenly tablets."

10 And Enoch began to recount from the books and said:

11 "I was born the seventh in the first week, while judgement and righteousness still endured.

12 And after me there shall arise in the second week great wickedness, and deceit shall have sprung up; and in it there shall be the first end.

13 And in it a man shall be saved; and after it is ended unrighteousness shall grow up, and a law shall be made for the sinners.

14 And after that in the third week at its close a man shall be elected as the plant of righteous judgement and his posterity shall become the plant of righteousness for evermore.

15 And after that in the fourth week, at its close, Visions of the holy and righteous shall be seen, and a law for all generations and an enclosure shall be made for them.

16 And after that in the fifth week, at its close, the house of glory and dominion shall be built for ever.

17 And after that in the sixth week all who live in it shall be blinded, and the hearts of all of them shall godlessly forsake wisdom.

18 And in it a man shall ascend; and at its close the house of dominion shall be burnt with fire, and the whole race of the chosen root shall be dispersed.

19 And after that in the seventh week shall an apostate generation arise, and many shall be its deeds, and all its deeds shall be apostate.

20 And at its close shall be elected, the elect righteous of the eternal plant of righteousness to receive sevenfold instruction concerning all His creation.

21 For who is there of all the children of men that is able to hear the voice of the Holy One without being troubled?

22 And who can think His thoughts?

23 And who is there that can behold all the works of heaven?

24 And how should there be one who could behold the heaven, and who is there that could understand the things of heaven and see a soul or a spirit and could tell thereof, or ascend and see all their ends and think them or do like them?

25 And who is there of all men that could know what is the breadth and the length of the earth, and to whom has been shown the measure of all of them?

26 Or is there any one who could discern the length of the heaven and how great is its height, and upon what it is founded, and how great is the number of the stars, and where all the luminaries rest?

27 And now I say unto you, my sons, love righteousness and walk therein; for the paths of righteousness are worthy of acceptance but the paths of unrighteousness shall suddenly be destroyed and vanish.

28 And to certain men of a generation shall the paths of violence and of death be revealed and they shall hold themselves afar from them, and shall not follow them.

29 And now I say unto you the righteous: Walk not in the paths of wickedness, nor in the paths of death, and draw not nigh to them, lest ye be destroyed.

30 But seek and choose for yourselves righteousness and an elect life, and walk in the paths of peace, and ye shall live and prosper.

31 And hold fast my words in the thoughts of your hearts and suffer them not to be effaced from your hearts; For I know that sinners will tempt men to evilly entreat wisdom so that no place may be found for her, and no manner of temptation may minish.

32 Woe to those who build unrighteousness and oppression and lay deceit as a foundation; For they shall be suddenly overthrown, and they shall have no peace.

33 Woe to those who build their houses with sin; For from all their foundations shall they be overthrown and by the sword shall they fall.

34 And those who acquire gold and silver in judgement suddenly shall perish.

35 Woe to you, ye rich, for ye have trusted in your riches and from your riches shall ye depart because ye have not remembered the Most High in the days of your riches.

36 Ye have committed blasphemy and unrighteousness, and have become ready for the day of slaughter, and the day of darkness and the day of the great judgement.

37 Thus I speak and declare unto you: He who hath created you will overthrow you and for your fall there shall be no compassion, and your Creator will rejoice at your destruction.

38 And your righteous ones in those days shall be a reproach to the sinners and the godless.

39 Oh that mine eyes were a cloud of waters that I might weep over you, and pour down my tears as a cloud of waters: That so I might rest from my trouble of heart!

40 Who has permitted you to practice reproaches and wickedness?

41 And so judgement shall overtake you, sinners.

42 Fear not the sinners, ye righteous; For again will the Lord deliver them into your hands, that ye may execute judgement upon them according to your desires.

43 Woe to you who fulminate anathemas which cannot be reversed: Healing shall therefore be far from you because of your sins.

44 Woe to you who requite your neighbor with evil; For ye shall be requited according to your works.

45 Woe to you, lying witnesses, and to those who weigh out injustice, for suddenly shall ye perish.

46 Woe to you, sinners, for ye persecute the righteous; for ye shall be delivered up and persecuted because of injustice, and heavy shall its yoke be upon you.

47 Be hopeful, ye righteous; for suddenly shall the sinners perish before you, and ye shall have lordship over them according to your desires.

48 And in the day of the tribulation of the sinners your children shall mount and rise as eagles, and higher than the vultures will be your nest, and ye shall ascend and enter the crevices of the earth, and the clefts of the rock for ever as coneys before the unrighteous, and the sirens shall sigh because of you and weep.

49 Wherefore fear not, ye that have suffered; For healing shall be your portion, and a bright light shall enlighten you, and the voice of rest ye shall hear from heaven.

50 Woe unto you, ye sinners, for your riches make you appear like the righteous but your hearts convict you of being sinners, and this fact shall be a testimony against you for a memorial of evil deeds.

51 Woe to you who devour the finest of the wheat and drink wine in large bowls, and tread under foot the lowly with your might.

52 Woe to you who drink water from every fountain; For suddenly shall ye be consumed and wither away because ye have forsaken the fountain of life.

53 Woe to you who work unrighteousness and deceit and blasphemy: It shall be a memorial against you for evil.

54 Woe to you, ye mighty, who with might oppress the righteous; For the day of your destruction is coming.

55 In those days many and good days shall come to the righteous in the day of your judgement."

Chapter 3
Wisdom of Enoch

1 Believe, ye righteous, that the sinners will become a shame nd perish in the day of unrighteousness.

2 Be it known unto you that the Most High is mindful of your destruction and the angels of heaven rejoice over your destruction.

3 What will ye do, ye sinners, and whither will ye flee on that day of judgement when ye hear the voice of the prayer of the righteous?

4 Yea, ye shall fare like unto them against whom this word shall be a testimony: "Ye have been companions of sinners."

5 And in those days the prayer of the righteous shall reach unto the Lord and for you the days of your judgement shall come.

6 And all the words of your unrighteousness shall be read out before the Great Holy One and your faces shall be covered with shame, and He will reject every work which is grounded on unrighteousness.

7 Woe to you, ye sinners, who live on the mid ocean and on the dry land whose remembrance is evil against you.

8 Woe to you who acquire silver and gold in unrighteousness and say: "We have become rich with riches and have possessions and have acquired everything we have desired. And now let us do what we purposed: For we have gathered silver and many are the husbandmen in our houses. And our granaries are full as with water."

9 Yea and like water your lies shall flow away for your riches shall not abide but speedily ascend from you; For ye have acquired it all in unrighteousness and ye shall be given over to a great curse.

10 And now I swear unto you, to the wise and to the foolish for ye shall have manifold experiences on the earth.

11 For ye men shall put on more adornments than a woman and colored garments more than a virgin; In royalty and in grandeur and in power, and in silver and in gold and in purple, and in splendor and in food they shall be poured out as water.

12 Therefore they shall be wanting in doctrine and wisdom and they shall perish thereby together with their possessions.

13 And with all their glory and their splendour, and in shame and in slaughter and in great destitution their spirits shall be cast into the furnace of fire.

14 I have sworn unto you, ye sinners, as a mountain has not become a slave and a hill does not become the handmaid of a woman.

15 Even so, sin has not been sent upon the earth but man of himself has created it, and under a great curse shall they fall who commit it.

16 And barrenness has not been given to the woman but on account of the deeds of her own hands she dies without children.

17 I have sworn unto you, ye sinners, by the Holy Great One; That all your evil deeds are revealed in the heavens and that none of your deeds of oppression are covered and hidden.

18 And do not think in your spirit nor say in your heart that ye do not know and that ye do not see that every sin is every day recorded in heaven in the presence of the Most High.

19 From henceforth ye know that all your oppression wherewith ye oppress is written down every day till the day of your judgement.

20 Woe to you, ye fools, for through your folly shall ye perish: And ye transgress against the wise, and so good hap shall not be your portion.

21 And now, know ye that ye are prepared for the day of destruction: Wherefore do not hope to live, ye sinners, but ye shall depart and die; for ye know no ransom; for ye are prepared for the day of the great judgement, for the day of tribulation and great shame for your spirits.

22 Woe to you, ye obstinate of heart, who work wickedness and eat blood: Whence have ye good things to eat and to drink and to be filled? From all the good things which the Lord the Most High has placed in abundance on the earth; therefore ye shall have no peace.

23 Woe to you who love the deeds of unrighteousness: Wherefore do ye hope for good hap unto yourselves? Know that ye shall be delivered into the hands of the righteous, and they shall cut off your necks and slay you, and have no mercy upon you.

24 Woe to you who rejoice in the tribulation of the righteous; For no grave shall be dug for you.

25 Woe to you who set at nought the words of the righteous; For ye shall have no hope of life.

26 Woe to you who write down lying and godless words; For they write down their lies that men may hear them and act godlessly towards neighbors.

27 Therefore they shall have no peace but die a sudden death.

28 Woe to you who work godlessness and glory in lying and extol them: Ye shall perish, and no happy life shall be yours.

29 Woe to them who pervert the words of uprightness and transgress the eternal law, and transform themselves into what they were not into sinners: They shall be trodden under foot upon the earth.

30 In those days make ready, ye righteous, to raise your prayers as a memorial, and place them as a testimony before the angels that they may place the sin of the sinners for a memorial before the Most High.

31 In those days the nations shall be stirred up and the families of the nations shall arise on the day of destruction.

32 And in those days the destitute shall go forth and carry off their children and they shall abandon them, so that their children shall perish through them: Yea, they shall abandon their children sucklings, and not return to them and shall have no pity on their beloved ones.

33 And again I swear to you, ye sinners, that sin is prepared for a day of unceasing bloodshed.

34 And they who worship stones, and grave images of gold and silver and wood and clay, and those who worship impure spirits and demons, and all kinds of idols not according to knowledge, shall get no manner of help from them.

35 And they shall become godless by reason of the folly of their hearts and their eyes shall be blinded through the fear of their hearts and through visions in their dreams.

36 Through these they shall become godless and fearful; For they shall have wrought all their work in a lie and shall have worshiped a stone: Therefore in an instant shall they perish.

37 But in those days blessed are all they who accept the words of wisdom, and understand them, and observe the paths of the Most High, and walk in the path of His righteousness, and become not godless with the godless; For they shall be saved.

38 Woe to you who spread evil to your neighbors; For you shall be slain in Sheol.

39 Woe to you who make deceitful and false measures, and who cause bitterness on the earth; For they shall thereby be utterly consumed.

40 Woe to you who build your houses through the grievous toil of others, and all their building materials are the bricks and stones of sin; I tell you ye shall have no peace.

41 Woe to them who reject the measure and eternal heritage of their fathers and whose souls follow after idols; For they shall have no rest.

42 Woe to them who work unrighteousness and help oppression, and slay their neighbours until the day of the great judgement.

43 For He shall cast down your glory and bring affliction on your hearts, and shall arouse His fierce indignation and destroy you all with the sword; And all the holy and righteous shall remember your sins.

44 And in those days in one place the fathers together with their sons shall be smitten and brothers one with another shall fall in death till the streams flow with their blood.

45 For a man shall not withhold his hand from slaying his sons and his sons sons, and the sinner shall not withhold his hand from his honored brother: From dawn till sunset they shall slay one another.

46 And the horse shall walk up to the breast in the blood of sinners and the chariot shall be submerged to its height.

47 In those days the angels shall descend into the secret places and gather together into one place all those who brought down sin and the Most High will arise on that day of judgement to execute great judgement amongst sinners.

48 And over all the righteous and holy He will appoint guardians from amongst the holy angels to guard them as the apple of an eye until He makes an end of all wickedness and all sin, and though the righteous sleep a long sleep, they have nought to fear.

49 And the children of the earth shall see the wise in security, and shall understand all the words of this book, and recognize that their riches shall not be able to save them in the overthrow of their sins.

50 Woe to you, Sinners, on the day of strong anguish, Ye who afflict the righteous and burn them with fire: Ye shall be requited according to your works.

51 Woe to you, ye obstinate of heart, who watch in order to devise wickedness: Therefore shall fear come upon you and there shall be none to help you.

52 Woe to you, ye sinners, on account of the words of your mouth, and on account of the deeds of your hands which your godlessness as wrought; In blazing flames burning worse than fire shall ye burn.

53 And now, know ye that from the angels He will inquire as to your deeds in heaven, from the sun and from the moon and from the stars in reference to your sins because upon the earth ye execute judgement on the righteous.

54 And He will summon to testify against you every cloud and mist and dew and rain; for they shall all be withheld because of you from descending upon you, and they shall be mindful of your sins.

55 And now give presents to the rain that it be not withheld from descending upon you, nor yet the dew, when it has received gold and silver from you that it may descend.

56 When the hoarfrost and snow with their chilliness, and all the snow storms with all their plagues fall upon you, in those days ye shall not be able to stand before them.

Chapter 4
Wisdom of Enoch

1 Observe the heaven, ye children of heaven, and every work of the Most High, and fear ye Him and work no evil in His presence.

2 If He closes the windows of heaven, and withholds the rain and the dew from descending on the earth on your account, what will ye do then?

3 And if He sends His anger upon you because of your deeds, ye cannot petition Him; for ye spake proud and insolent words against His righteousness: therefore ye shall have no peace.

4 And see ye not the sailors of the ships, how their ships are tossed to and fro by the waves, and are shaken by the winds, and are in sore trouble?

5 And therefore do they fear because all their goodly possessions go into the sea with them, and they have evil forebodings of heart that the sea will swallow them and they will perish therein.

6 Are not the entire sea and all its waters, and all its movements, the work of the Most High, and has He not set limits to its doings, and confined it throughout by the sand?

7 And at His reproof it is afraid and dries up, and all its fish die and all that is in it; But ye sinners that are on the earth fear Him not.

8 Has He not made the heaven and the earth, and all that is therein?

9 Who has given understanding and wisdom to everything that moves on the earth and in the sea?

10 Do not the sailors of the ships fear the sea? Yet sinners fear not the Most High.

11 In those days when He hath brought a grievous fire upon you, whither will ye flee, and where will ye find deliverance?

12 And when He launches forth His Word against you will you not be affrighted and fear? And all the luminaries shall be affrighted with great fear and all the earth shall be affrighted and tremble and be alarmed.

13 And all the angels shall execute their commandst and shall seek to hide themselves from the presence of the Great Glory, and the children of earth shall tremble and quake; and ye sinners shall be cursed for ever, and ye shall have no peace.

14 Fear ye not, ye souls of the righteous and be hopeful ye that have died in righteousness.

15 And grieve not if your soul into Sheol has descended in grief, and that in your life your body fared not according to your goodness but wait for the day of the judgement of sinners and for the day of cursing and chastisement.

16 And yet when ye die the sinners speak over you: "As we die, so die the righteous, and what benefit do they reap for their deeds? Behold, even as we, so do they die in grief and darkness and what have they more than we? From henceforth we are equal. And what will they receive and what will they see for ever? Behold, they too have died, And henceforth for ever shall they see no light."

17 I tell you, "Ye sinners, ye are content to eat and drink, and rob and sin, and strip men naked, and acquire wealth and see good days. Have ye seen the righteous how their end falls out, that no manner of violence is found in them till their death?

18 Nevertheless they perished and became as though they had not been, and their spirits descended into Sheol in tribulation."

Chapter 5
Wisdom of Enoch

1 Another book which Enoch wrote for his son Methuselah and for those who will come after him, and keep the law in the last days.

2 Ye who have done good shall wait for those days till an end is made of those who work evil; and an end of the might of the transgressors.

3 And wait ye indeed till sin has passed away, for their names shall be blotted out of the book of life and out of the holy books, and their seed shall be destroyed for ever, and their spirits shall be slain, and they shall cry and make lamentation in a place that is a chaotic wilderness, and in the fire shall they burn; for there is no earth there.

4 And I saw there something like an invisible cloud; for by reason of its depth I could not look over, and I saw a flame of fire blazing brightly, and things like shining mountains circling and sweeping to and fro.

5 And I asked one of the holy angels who was with me and said unto him: "What is this shining thing? For it is not a heaven but only the flame of a blazing fire, and the voice of weeping and crying and lamentation and strong pain."

6 And he said unto me: "This place which thou seest here are cast the spirits of sinners and blasphemers, and of those who work wickedness, and of those who pervert everything that the Lord hath spoken through the mouth of the prophets the things that shall be.

7 For some of them are written and inscribed above in the heaven, in order that the angels may read them and know that which shall befall the sinners, and the spirits of the humble, and of those who have afflicted their bodies, and been recompensed by God.

8 And of those who have been put to shame by wicked men: Who love God and loved neither gold nor silver nor any of the good things which are in the world, but gave over their bodies to torture.

9 Who, since they came into being, longed not after earthly food, but regarded everything as a passing breath, and lived accordingly, and the Lord tried them much, and their spirits were found pure so that they should bless His name.

10 And all the blessings destined for them I have recounted in the books.

11 And he hath assigned them their recompense, because they have been found to be such as loved heaven more than their life in the world, and though they were trodden under foot of wicked men and experienced abuse and reviling from them and were put to shame, yet they blessed Me.

12 And now I will summon the spirits of the good who belong to the generation of light, and I will transform those who were born in darkness, who in the flesh were not recompensed with such honor as their faithfulness deserved.

13 And I will bring forth in shining light those who have loved My holy name, and I will seat each on the throne of his honor.

14 And they shall be resplendent for times without number; for righteousness is the judgement of God; for to the faithful He will give faithfulness in the habitation of upright paths.

15 And they shall see those who were, born in darkness led into darkness, while the righteous shall be resplendent.

16 And the sinners shall cry aloud and see them resplendent, and they indeed will go where days and seasons are prescribed for them."

Chapter 6
Revelation of Enoch

1 I swear unto you that in heaven the angels remember you for good before the glory of the Great One: and your names are written before the glory of the Great One.

2 Be hopeful; for aforetime ye were put to shame through ill and affliction; but now ye shall shine as the lights of heaven, ye shall shine and ye shalll be seen, and the portals of heaven shall be opened to you.

3 And in your cry, cry for judgement, and it shall appear to you; for all your tribulation shall be visited on the rulers, and on all who helped those who plundered you.

4 Be hopeful, and cast not away your hopes for ye shall have great joy as the angels of heaven.

5 What shall ye be obliged to do?

6 Ye shall not have to hide on the day of the great judgement and ye shall not be found as sinners, and the eternal judgement shall be far from you for all the generations of the world.

7 And now fear not, ye righteous, when ye see the sinners growing strong and prospering in their ways, be not companions with them, but keep afar from their violence; For ye shall become companions of the hosts of heaven.

8 And, although the sinners say: "All our sins shall not be searched out and be written down," nevertheless they shall write down all your sins every day.

9 And now I show unto you that light and darkness, day and night, see all your sins.

10 Be not godless in your hearts, and lie not and alter not the words of uprightness, nor charge with lying the words of the Holy Great One, nor take account of your idols; for all your lying and all your godlessness issue not in righteousness but in great sin.

11 And now I know this mystery, that sinners will alter and pervert the words of righteousness in many ways, and will speak wicked words, and lie, and practice great deceits, and write books concerning their words.

12 But when they write down truthfully all my words in their languages, and do not change or minish ought from my words but write them all down truthfully all that I first testified concerning them.

13 Then, I know another mystery, that books will be given to the righteous and the wise to become a cause of joy and uprightness and much wisdom.

14 And to them shall the books be given, and they shall believe in them and rejoice over them and then shall all the righteous who have learnt therefrom all the paths of uprightness be recompensed.

15 In those days the Lord bade to summon and testify to the children of earth concerning their wisdom: "Show unto them; for ye are their guides and a recompense over the whole earth.

16 For I and My son will be united with them for ever in the paths of uprightness in their lives; and ye shall have peace: rejoice, ye children of uprightness. Amen."

EXTRAS

The Book of the Giants

The Book of the Giants was published in not less than six or seven languages. From the original Syriac the Greek and Middle Persian versions were made. The Sogdian edition was probably derived from the Middle Persian, the Uygur from the Sogdian. There is no trace of a Parthian text. The book may have existed in Coptic. The presence of names such as Sām and Narīmān in the Arabic version proves that it had been translated from the Middle Persian. To the few surviving fragments (texts A-G) I have added two excerpts, the more important of which (H) probably derives from a Syriac epitome of the book. Naturally, Manichæan authors quoted the book frequently, but there is only one direct citation by a non-Manichæan writer (text O). With the exception of text O, all the passages referring to the *Book of the Giants* (texts J-T) go back to Syriac writings (apparently). They are, therefore, to be treated as quotations from the Syriac edition. E.g. the Parthian text N is not the product of a Parthian writer who might have employed a Parthian version of the book, but was translated from a Syriac treatise whose author cited the Syriac text.

In their journey across Central Asia the stories of the *Book of the Giants* were influenced by local traditions. Thus, the translation of Ohya as Sām had in its train the introduction of myths appertaining to that Iranian hero; this explains the "immortality" of Sā(h)m according to text I. The country of *Aryān-Vēžan* = *Airyana Vaējah*, in text G (26), is a similar innovation. The "Kögmän mountains" in text B may reflect the "Mount Hermon". The progeny of the fallen angels was confined in thirty-six towns (text S). Owing to the introduction of the Mount Sumeru, this number was changed (in Sogdiana) to *thirty-two* (text G, 22): "the heaven of Indra . . . is situated between the four peaks (cf. G 21) of the Meru, and consists of *thirty-two* cities of devas" (Eitel, *Handb. Chinese Buddhism*, 148, on *Trayastriṃśat*).

Manuscript Mapping Key
(bed) = damaged letters, or uncertain readings,
[bed] = suggested restorations of missing letters.
= visible, but illegible letters.
[. . .] = estimated number of missing letters.
[ ] = a lacuna of undetermined extent.
(84)] = same, at the beginning of a line.
[(85 = same, at the end of a line.

In the translation parentheses are employed for explanatory remarks.

Bolded text of the translation fragments are of great importance and correlation with the books of Enoch.

NOTE: The text from multiple of these manuscripts is *badly damaged* but between the various versions of the book in different languages we have a general picture of what the Book of Giants is discussing if the book's very title isn't enough for the reader alone. Logical estimates according to the historical texts which tell of these giants living, seem to be around 3500BC and the manuscripts (presumably) being copied several times throughout the ages (considering any scribe would find copying an epic like this more than just a "great job," they probably did it for free; which explains why so many manuscripts exist of the book) are more than likely around 3000+ years old.

Translation to English

[INTRODUCTION]

(*Frg. c*) . . . hard . . . arrow . . . bow, he that . . . Sām said: "Blessed be . . . had [he ?] seen this, he would not have died." Then Shahmīzād said to Sām, his [son]: "All that Māhawai . . ., is spoilt (?)." Thereupon he said to . . . "We are . . . until (10) . . . and . . . (13) . . . that are in (?) the fiery hell (?) . . . As my father, Virōgdād, was . . ." Shahmīzād said: "It is true what he says. **He says one of thousands of giants.** For one of thousands . . . .". Sām thereupon began . . . Māhawai, too, in many places . . . (20) until to that place he might escape (1) and . . .

(*Frg. j*) . . . Virōgdād . . . **Hōbābiš (a giant) robbed Ahr (a mortal man) of Naxtag, his wife.** Thereupon the giants began to kill each other and [to abduct their wives]. The creatures, too, began to kill each other. Sām . . . before the sun, one hand in the air, the other (30) . . . whatever he obtained, to his brother . . . . imprisoned . . . (34) . . . over Taxtag. To the angels . . . from heaven. Taxtag to . . . Taxtag threw (*or*: was thrown) into the water. Finally (?) . . . in his sleep Taxtag saw three signs, [one portending . . .], one woe and flight, and one . . . annihilation. Narīmān saw a gar[den full of] (40) trees in rows. Two hundred . . . came out, the trees. . . .

(*Frg. l*) **Enoch, the apostle**, . . . [gave] a message to [the demons and their] children: To you . . . not peace. [The judgment on you is] that you shall be bound for the sins you have committed. You shall see the destruction of your children. ruling for a hundred and twenty [years] . . . . (50) . . . wild ass, ibex . . . ram, goat (?), gazelle, . . . oryx, of each two hundred, a pair . . . the other wild beasts, birds, and animals and their wine [shall be] six thousand jugs . . . irritation(?) of water (?) . . . and their oil shall be . . .

(*Frg. k*) . . . father . . . nuptials (?) . . . until the completion of his . . . in fighting . . . (60) . . . and in the nest(?) Ohya and Ahya . . . he said to his brother: "get up and . . . we will take what our father has ordered us to. The pledge we have given . . . battle." **And the giants fought them together** . . . (67) "[Not the] . . . of the lion, but the . . . on his . . . [Not the] . . . of the rainbow, but the bow . . . firm. Not the sharpness of the blade, [but] (70) the strength of the ox (?). Not the . . . eagle, but his wings. Not the . . . gold, but the brass that hammers it. Not the proud [ruler], but the diadem on his [head. Not] the splendid cypress, but the . . . **giants of the mountain** . . .

(*Frg. g*) . . . Not he that engages in quarrels, but he that is true in his speech. Not the evil fruit(?), but the poison in it. (80) [Not they that] are placed (?) in the skies but the God [of all] worlds. Not the servant is proud, but [the lord] that is above him. Not one that is sent . . ., but the man that sent him". Thereupon Narīmān . . . said . . . (86) . . . And (in) **another place I saw those that were weeping for the ruin that had befallen them, and whose cries and laments rose up to heaven.** (90) And also I saw another place [where there were] tyrants and rulers . . . in great number, who had lived in sin and evil deeds, when . . . (Note here that this passage is in the style of Enoch and is likely one of the many books Enoch gave to Methuselah to "preserve even unto future generations.")

(*Frg. i*) . . . many men and women were killed, **four hundred thousand Righteous . . . with fire, naphtha, and brimstone . . . And the angels veiled (*or:*covered, *or:* protected, *or:* moved out of sight) Enoch.** *Electae et auditrices* (100) . . . and ravished them. They chose beautiful women, and demanded . . . them in marriage. Sordid . . . (103) . . . all . . . carried off . . . severally they were subjected to tasks and services. And they . . . from each city . . . and were, ordered to serve the . . . The Mesenians [were directed] to prepare, the Khūzians to sweep [and] (110) water, the Persians to . . .

[On the Five Elements]

(*Frg. e*) (112) . . . slaying . . . righteous . . . good deeds . . . . elements. The crown, the diadem, [the garland, and] the garment (of Light). The seven demons. Like a blacksmith [who] binds (*or:*shuts, fastens) and looses (*or:* opens, detaches) . . . . who from the seeds of . . . . and serves the king . . . . (120) . . . offends . . . when weeping . . . with mercy . . . hand . . . (125) . . . the Pious gave . . . ? . . . presents. Some buried the idols. The Jews did good and evil. Some make their god half demon, half god . . . (130) killing . . . the seven demons . . . eye . . .

(*Frg. b*) . . . various colours that by . . . and bile. If. . . . from the five elements. As if (it were) a means not to die, they fill themselves with food and drink. Their (140) garment is . . . this corpse . . . and not firm . . . Its ground is not firm . . . Like . . . (146) . . . imprisoned [in this corpse], in bones, nerves, [flesh], veins, and skin, and entered herself [= *Āz*] into it. Then he (= Man) cries out, over (?) sun and moon, the Just God's (150) two flames . . . ? . . ., over the elements, the trees and the animals. But God [Zrwān ?], in each epoch, sends apostles: Šīt[īl, Zarathushtra,] Buddha, Christ, . . .

(*Frg. h*) . . . evil-intentioned . . . from where . . . he came. The Misguided recognize the five elements, [the five kinds of] trees, the five (kinds of) animals.

(160) ... On the Hearers>

... we receive ... from Mani, the Lord, ... the Five Commandments to ... the Three Seals ... (164) ... living ... profession ... and wisdom ... moon. Rest from the power (*or*: deceit) ... own. And keep measured the mixture (?) ... trees and wells, in two ... (170) water, and fruit, milk, ... he should not offend his brother. The wise [Hearer] who like unto juniper [leaves ...

(*Frg. f*) ... much profit. Like a farmer ... who sows seed .. in many ... The Hearer who ... knowledge, is like unto a man that threw (the dish called) *frōšag*(180) [into] milk(?). It became hard, not ... The part that ruin ... at first heavy. Like ... first ... is honoured ... might shine ... (188) six days. The Hearer who gives alms (to the Elect), is like unto a poor (190) man that presents his daughter to the king; he reaches (a position of) great honour. In the body of the Elect the (food given to to him as) alms is purified in the same manner as a ... that by fire and wind ... beautiful clothes on a clean body ... turn ...

(*Frg. a*) ... witness ... fruit ... (200) ... tree ... like firewood ... like a grain (?) ... radiance. The Hearer in [the world ?], (and) the alms within the Church, are like unto a ship [on the sea] : the towing-line (is) in the hand of [the tower] on shore, the sailor (210) is [on board the ship]. The sea is the world, the ship is [the ..., the ... is the ?al]ms, the tower is [the ... ?], the towing-line (?) is the Wisdom. ... ... (214) ... The Hearer ... is like unto the branch (?) of a fruitless [tree] ... fruitless ... and the Hearers ... fruit that ... (220) pious deeds. [The Elect,] the Hearer, and Vahman, are like unto three brothers to whom some [possessions] were left by their father: a piece of land, ..., seed. They became partners ... they reap and ... The Hearer ... like ...

(*Frg. d*) ... an image (?) of the king, cast of gold ... (230) ... the king gave presents. The Hearer that copies a book, is like unto a sick man that gave his ... to a ... man. The Hearer that gives [his] daughter to the church, is like ... pledge, who (= father ?) gave his son to ... learn ... to ... father, pledge ... (240) ... Hearer. Again, the Hearer ... is like .... stumble ... is purified. To ... the soul from the Church, is like unto the wife of the soldier (*or*: Roman) who ... infantrist, one shoe ... who, however, with a denarius ... was. The wind tore out one ... he was abashed ... from the ground ... ground ...

(*Frg. m*) ... (250) ... sent ... The Hearer that makes one ..., is like unto [a compassionate mother] who had seven sons ... the enemy [killed] all ... The Hearer that ... piety ... (258) ... a well. One [on the shore of] the sea, one in the boat. (260) [He that is on] shore, tows(?) him that is [in the boat].1 He that is in the boat. ... sea. Upwards to ... like .. ? .. like a pearl ... diadem ...

(*Frg. M* 911) . . . Church. Like unto a man that . . . fruit and flowers . . . then they praise . . . fruitful tree . . . (270) . . . [Like unto a man] that bought a piece of land. [On that] piece of land [there was] a well, [and in that well a bag] full of drachmas . . . the king was filled with wonder . . . share . . . pledge . . .

(*Frg. n*) . . . numerous . . . Hearer. At . . . like unto a garment . . . (280) like . . . to the master . . . like . . . and a blacksmith. The goldsmith . . . to honour, the blacksmith to . . . one to . . .

B. Uygur

LeCoq, *Türk. Man.*, iii, 23. Bang, *Muséon*, xliv, 13-17. Order of pages according to LeCoq (the phot. publ. by Bang seems to support LeCoq's opinion).

(*First page*) . . . fire was going to come out. And [I saw] that the sun was at the point of rising, and that [his ?] centre (*ordu*) without increasing (? *ašïlmatïn* ?) above was going to start rolling. Then came a voice from the air above. Calling me, it spoke thus: "Oh son of Virōgdād, your affairs are lamentable (?). More than this you shall [not] see. Do not die now prematurely, but turn quickly back from here." And again, besides this (voice), I heard the voice of Enoch, the apostle, from the south, without, however, seeing him at all. Speaking my name very lovingly, he called. And downwards from . . . then

(*Second page*) . . . " . . for the closed door of the sun will open, the sun's light and heat will descend and set your wings alight. You will burn and die," said he. Having heard these words, I beat my wings and quickly flew down from the air. I looked back: Dawn had . . . ., with the light of the sun it had come to rise over the Kögmän mountains. And again a voice came from above. Bringing the command of Enoch, the apostle, it said: "I call you, Virōgdād, . . . I know . . . his direction . . . you . . . you . . . Now quickly . . . people . . . also . . .

C. Sogdian

M 648. Small scrap from the centre of a page. Order of pages uncertain.

(*First page*) . . . I shall see. Thereupon now S[āhm, the giant] was [very] angry, and laid hands on M[āhawai, the giant], with the intention: I shall . . . and kill [you]. Then . . . the other g[iants . . .

(*Second page*) . . . do not be afraid, for . . . [Sā]hm, the giant, will want to [kill] you, but I shall not let him . . . I myself shall damage . . . Thereupon Māhawai, the g[iant], . . . was satisfied . . .

D. Middle-Persian

Published *Sb.P.A.W.*, 1934, p. 29.

... outside ... and ... left .... read the dream we have seen. Thereupon Enoch thus .... and the trees that came out, those are the Egrēgoroi (*'yr*), and the giants that came out of the women. And ..... over ... pulled out ... over ...

E. Sogdian

T iii 282. Order of pages uncertain.

(*First page*) ... [when] they saw the apostle, ... before the apostle ... those demons that were [timid], were very, very glad at seeing the apostle. All of them assembled before him. Also, of those that were tyrants and criminals, they were [worried] and much afraid. Then ...

(*Second page*) ... not to ... Thereupon those powerful demons spoke thus to the pious apostle : If .... by us any (further) sin [will] not [be committed ?], my lord, why ? .... you have ... and weighty injunction ...

F. Middle-Persian

T ii D ii 164. Six fragmentary columns, from the middle of a page. Order of columns uncertain. Instead of A///B///CDEF, it might have been: BCDEFA, or even CDEF///A///B.

(*Col. A*) ... poverty ... **[those who] harassed the happiness of the Righteous, on that account they shall fall into eternal ruin and distress, into that Fire, the mother of all conflagrations and the foundation of all ruined tyrants. And when these sinful misbegotten sons of ruin in those crevices** and ....

(*Col. B*) ... you have not been better. In error you thought you would this false power eternally. You ... all this iniquity ...

(*Col. C*) ... you that call to us with the voice of falsehood. Neither did we reveal ourselves on *your* account, so that *you* could see us, nor thus .... ourselves through the praise and greatness that to us .... -given to you ..., but ...

(Col. D) . . . sinners . . . . . is visible, where out of this fire your soul will be prepared (for the transfer) to eternal ruin (?). And as for you, sinful misbegotten sons of the Wrathful Self, confounders of the true words of that Holy One, disturbers of the actions of Good Deed, aggressors upon Piety, . . . -ers of the Living. . . ., who their . . .

(Col. E) . . . and on brilliant wings they shall fly and soar further outside and above that Fire, and shall gaze into its depth and height. And those Righteous that will stand around it, outside and above, they themselves shall have power over that Great Fire, and over everything in it. . . . . . blaze . . . . souls that . . .

(Col. F) . . . they are purer and stronger [than the] Great Fire of Ruin that sets the worlds ablaze. They shall stand around it, outside and above, and splendour shall shine over them. Further outside and above it they shall fly (?) after those souls that may try to escape from the Fire. And that . . . .

G. Sogdian

T ii. Two folios (one only publ. here; the other contains a *wyδβ'γ cn pš'qt δywtyy* "Discourse on the Nephīlīm-demons"). Head-lines: *R: pš'n prβ'r* ". . . pronouncement", *V: iv fryštyt δn CC* "**The four angels with the two hundred** [demons . . . ". (Presumably this is where Enoch is addressing the 200 fallen angel leaders who petitioned him to take their case to God. It also coincides with the text later on revealing that four angels imprisoned multiple demons but precisely how many is not specified.)

. . . they took and imprisoned all the helpers that were in the heavens. **And the angels themselves descended from the heaven to the earth. And (when) the two hundred demons saw those angels, they were much afraid and worried. They assumed the shape of men and hid themselves. Thereupon the angels forcibly removed the men from the demons, (10) laid them aside, and put watchers over them** . . . . the giants . . . . were sons . . . with each other in bodily union . . . . with each other self- . . . . and the . . . . that had been born to them, they forcibly removed them from the demons. And they led one half of them (20) eastwards, and the other half westwards, on the skirts of four huge mountains, towards the foot of the **Sumeru mountain**, into thirty-two towns which the Living Spirit had prepared for them in the beginning. And one calls (that place) Aryān-waižan. And those men are (*or:* were) . . . . in the first arts and crafts. (30) . . . . they made . . . the angels . . . and to the demons . . . **they went to fight. And those two hundred demons fought a hard battle with the four angels, until the angels used fire, naphtha, and brimstone** . . . .

EXCERPTS

H. Sogdian

T ii S 20. Sogdian script. Two folios. Contents similar to the "Kephalaia". Only about a quarter (I R i-17) publ. here. The following chapter has as headline: *''yšt š'nš'y cnn 'β[c'n]pδ[yh w]prs* = Here begins: Šanšai's question the world. Init. *rty tym ZK š'nš'[y] [cnn] m'rm'ny rwyšny pr'yš[t'kw w'nkw ']prs' 'yn'k 'βc'npδ ZY kw ZKh mrtymyt ('skw'nt)* oo *ckn'c pyδ'r ''zy mrch 'zyyr'nt* = And again Šanšai asked the Light Apostle: this world where mankind lives, why does one call it birth-death (*saṃsāra*, Chin. *shêng-szŭ*).

. . . and what they had seen in the heavens among the gods, and also what they had seen in hell, their native land, and furthermore what they had seen on earth,—**all that they began to teach (*hendiadys*) to the men**. To Šahmīzād two(?) sons were borne by . . . . One of them he named "Ohya"; in Sogdian he is called "Sāhm, the giant". And again a second son [was born] to him. He named him "Ahya"; its Sogdian (equivalent) is "Pāt-Sāhm". **As for the remaining giants, they were born to the other demons** and Yakṣas. (*Colophon*) Completed: (the chapter on) "**The Coming of the two hundred Demons**".

I. Sogdian

M 500 n. Small fragment.

. . . . manliness, in powerful tyranny, he (*or*: you ?) shall not die". The giant Sāhm and his brother will live eternally. For in the whole world in power and strength, and in . . . .

QUOTATIONS AND ALLUSIONS

J. Middle-Persian

T ii D ii 120, V ii 1-5: and in the coming of the two hundred demons there are two paths: the hurting speech, and the hard labour; these (belong, *or*: lead) to hell.

K. Sogdian

M 363.

(*First page*) ... before ... they were. And all the ... fulfilled their tasks lawfully. Now, they became excited and irritated for the following reason: namely, **the two hundred demons came down to the sphere from the high heaven**, and the ....

(*Second page*) ... in the world they became excited and irritated. For their life-lines and the connections of their Pneumatic Veins are joined to the sphere. (*Colophon*) Completed: the exposition of the three worlds. (*Head-line*) Here begins: the coming of Jesus and [his bringing] the religion to Adam and Šitil. ... you should care and ...

L. Coptic

Kephalaia, 171 16-19: Earthquake and malice happened in the watchpost of the Great King of Honour, namely the Egrēgoroi who arose at the time when they were .... and **there descended those who were sent to confound them**. (Genesis 11)

M. Coptic

Kephalaia, 92 24-31: Now attend and behold how the Great King of Honour who is ἔννοια, is in the third heaven. He is ... with the wrath ... and a rebellion ..., when malice and wrath arose in his camp, namely the **Egrēgoroi of Heaven who in his watch-district (rebelled and) descended to the earth. They did all deeds of malice. They revealed the arts in the world, and the mysteries of heaven to the men. Rebellion and ruin came about on the earth** ...

N. Parthian

M 35, lines 21-36. Fragment of a treatise entitled *'rdhng wyfr's* = Commentary on (Mani's opus)*Ārdahang*.

And the story about the Great Fire: like unto (the way in which) the Fire, with powerful wrath, swallows this world and enjoys it; like unto (the way in which) this fire that is in the body, swallows the exterior fire that is (*lit.* comes) in fruit and food, and enjoys it. Again, like unto (the story in which) two brothers who found a treasure, and a pursuer lacerated each other, and they died; like unto (the fight in which) Ohya, Lewyātīn (= Leviathan), and Raphael lacerated each other, and they vanished; like unto (the story in which) a lion cub, a calf in a wood (*or*: on a meadow), and a fox lacerated each other, [and they vanished, *or*: died]. Thus [the Great Fire swallows, etc.] both of the fires. . . .

M 740. Another copy of this text.

O. Arabic, from Middle Persian ?

Al-Ghaḍanfar (Abū Isḥāq Ibr. b. Muḥ. al-Tibrīzī, middle of thirteenth century), in Sachau's edition of Beruni's *Āthār al-bāqiyah*, Intr., p. xiv: The *Book of the Giants*, by Mani of Babylon, is filled with stories about these (antediluvian) giants, amongst whom Sām and Narīmān.

P. Coptic

Keph. 9323-28: On account of the malice and rebellion that had arisen in the watch-post of the Great King of Honour, **namely the Egrēgoroi who from the heavens had descended to the earth,—on their account the four angels received their orders: they bound the Egrēgoroi with eternal fetters in the prison of the Dark(?), their sons were destroyed upon the earth.**

Q. Coptic

Manich. Psalm-book, ed. Allberry, 1427-9: The Righteous who were burnt in the fire, they endured. This multitude that were wiped out, four thousand . . . . Enoch also, the Sage, the transgressors being . . .

R. Coptic

Man. Homil., ed. Polotsky, 6818-19: . . . evil. 400,000 Righteous were slain by the giants and many more . . . . **the years of Enoch** . . .

S. Coptic

Keph., 117 1-9: **Before the Egrēgoroi rebelled and descended from heaven, a prison had been built for them in the depth of the earth beneath the mountains.** Before the sons of the giants were born who knew not Righteousness and Piety among themselves, thirty-six towns had been prepared and erected, so that the sons of the giants should live in them, they that come to beget . . . . who live a thousand years.

T. Parthian

291a. Order of pages unknown.

(*First page*) . . . mirror . . . image. . . . distributed. The men . . . and Enoch was veiled (= moved out of sight). They took . . . Afterwards, with donkey-goads . . . . slaves, and waterless trees (?). **Then the arch angels Michael, Raphel, Gabriel, and Istrael . . . and imprisoned the demons**. And of them . . . . seven and twelve. (Possibly a numerical indication as to how many demons the archangels imprisoned?)

(*Second page*) . . . three thousand two hundred and eighty- . . . the beginning of King Vištāsp.. . . . in the palace he flamed forth (*or*: in the brilliant palace). And at night . . ., then to the broken gate . . . men . . . physicians, merchants, farmers, . . . at sea. ? . . . armoured he came out . . .

U. Parthian

T ii D 58. From the end (. . . *r š t*) of a hymn.

. . . gifts. A peaceful sovereign [was] King Vištāsp, [in Aryā]n-Waižan Wahman and Zarēl . . . . The sovereign's queen, Khudōs, received the Faith, the prince . . . They have secured (a place in) the (heavenly) hall, and quietude for ever and ever . . .

V. Sogdian

M 692. Small fragment. Order of pages uncertain.

(*First page*) . . . because . . . the House of the Gods, eternal joy, and good . . ? . . For so it is said: at that time . . . Yima was . . . in the world. And at the time of the new moon (?) . . . . the blessed denizens of the world . . . all assembled . . . all . . .

(*Second page*) . . . they offered five garlands in homage. And Yima accepted those garlands . . . And those . . . that . . . . and great kingship . . . was his. And on . . . them . . . . And acclamations . . . And from that pious (?) . . . he placed the garlands on his head . . . the denizens of the world . . .

Evidence of Giants

Fossilized remains of giant human skeletons have been found all around the world. Ranging in size, many of them have been recovered with giant weapons, armor, and strange artifacts dubbed OOPARTS (Out of Place Artifacts). The current worldview model for humanity doesn't support the existence of a giant human race (according to evolution). These enormous ancient human beings were worshipped throughout various world religions of which tell of many of them slaying dragons. It is important to note that the term "dragon" was replaced by the word "dinosaur" in 1871 by Sir. Edward Owen. Hence, any reference in ancient literature to dragons, is a reference to dinosaurs according to the ontology of the word change associations involved. The following is a brief report of recovered giant fossilized human remains of which most end up in private collections of the elite of society save a few who have found their way to museums around the world. Although in recent years many of these museums have been selling these remains to private collectors for large sums of money their discoveries remain documented and undisputed by reasonable scholars without hidden agendas. Take a look at the evidence and decide for yourself if there were "Giants on the earth in those days." - Genesis 6:4

Perhaps the best place to start off with providing evidence of the existence of giant human beings is Crete. Crete was once known in old times as Arcadia. The Greek historian Herodotus had written about another historian, Eustathius who had said that Arcadia was once called Gigantis, or "The Land of Giants," because of the giants who had formerly lived there. It was also known as the Greek Garden of Eden. This connection between Arcadia, giants, and to the Garden of Eden makes sense, because the 4th century Roman author Servius in his Commentary on the Eneid says, that the Arcadians often reached the age of 300 years.—Grotius.

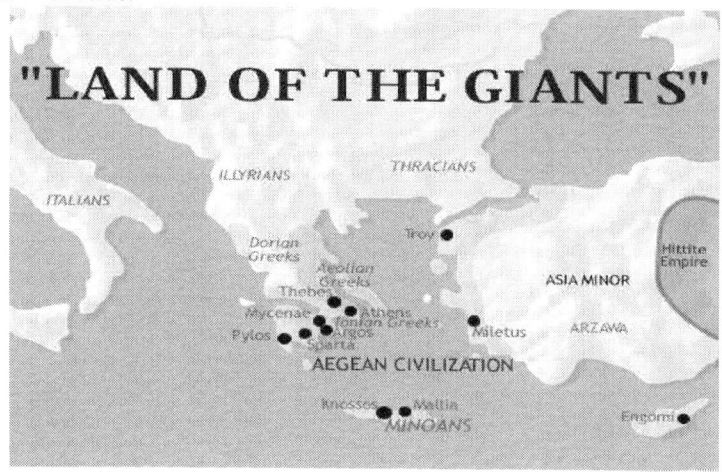

Several of the world's most influential authors all throughout history verify these accounts of giants, gods, and the island of Crete. People such as Diodorus Siculus, Pliny, Strabo, Plutarch, and Plato, just to name a few. In addition to these historical accounts by some of the world's most trusted authorities, there is also the science with real life giant bones that have been found on Crete. In fact, the largest bones that have ever been found were discovered on this very same island, which may prove this was truly the home or the Land of Giants.

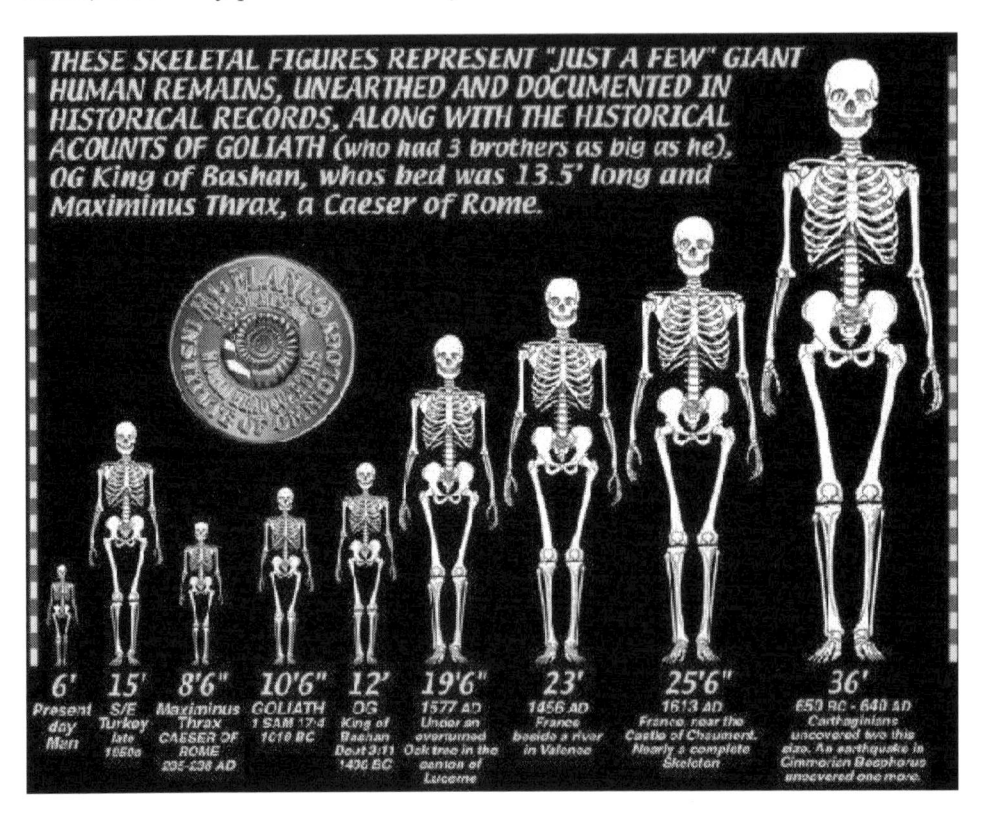

THESE SKELETAL FIGURES REPRESENT "JUST A FEW" GIANT HUMAN REMAINS, UNEARTHED AND DOCUMENTED IN HISTORICAL RECORDS, ALONG WITH THE HISTORICAL ACOUNTS OF GOLIATH (who had 3 brothers as big as he), OG King of Bashan, whos bed was 13.5' long and Maximinus Thrax, a Caeser of Rome.

6'	15'	8'6"	10'6"	12'	19'6"	23'	25'6"	36'
Present day Man	S/E Turkey late 1050s	Maximinus Thrax CAESER OF ROME 235-238 AD	GOLIATH 1 SAM 17:4	OG King of Bashan Deut 3:11 1406 BC	1577 AD Under an overturned Oak tree in the canton of Lucerne	1456 AD France beside a river in Valence	1613 AD France near the Castle of Chaumont. Nearly a complete Skeleton	650 BC - 640 AD Carthaginians uncovered two this size. An earthquake in Cimmerian Bosphorus uncovered one more.

As you can see, the evidence and fossil remains of giant humans was and is not the problem. Reconciling their existence, however, is the problem. If we accept the biblical account that fallen angels produced giant children with women and believe the bible on this accord, then we're all the better for it. Evolutionary 'giantism' doesn't work out in the real world. It doesn't explain why we don't see any 23 foot tall men walking around today. It just doesn't happen. Furthermore, the DNA of these giant skeletons is pretty interesting too. It's 'more pure' according to geneticists who have analyzed it. To date, around 400 giant skeletons have been unearthed. When we look at history recording giants it seems to make so much more sense than the evolutionary explanation. It's logical to believe the bible's accounts of giants in this case. The evidence persists that the holy scriptures are right in this regard. Skeletons never lie.

During the Cretan war from 205–200 BC a massive giant skeleton was discovered on the island. **This giant was measured at the length of thirty-three cubits, which equates to nearly 42 feet.** The Roman Lucius Flaccus was a notable eye witness to the gigantic bones, and the Greek writer under Roman Emperor Hadrian, Phlegon of Tralles also mentions the discovery of several giant skeletons. In the included chart of giant fossilized remains findings around the world features the 36 foot skeleton found by the Carthaginians.

In the The Geography of Strabo, Volume 1 By Strabo, he writes about these giants that were discovered in city founded by the biblical Corinthians who used to reside in the modern day island of Crete;

"Somewhere in this neighbourhood is the mountain Bermius,2 which was formerly in the possession of the Briges, a Thracian nation, some of whom passed over to Asia and were called by another name, Phrygians (Phryges). After Thessalonica follows the remaining part of the Therman Gulf, extending to Canastneum. This is a promontory of a peninsula form, and is opposite to Magnesia. Pallene is the name of the peninsula. It has an isthmus 5 stadia in width, with a ditch cut across it. There is a city on the peninsula, formerly called Potidsna, founded by the Corinthians, but afterwards it was called Cassandria, from king Cassander, who restored it after it was demolished. It is a circuit of 570 stadia round the peninsula by sea. **Here giants were said to have lived, and the region to have been called Phlegra. Some consider this to be a mere fable, but others, with greater probability on their side, see implied in it the existence of a barbarous and lawless race of people who once occupied the country**, but who were destroyed by Hercules on his return home, after the capture of Troy. Here also the Trojan women are said to have committed the destructive act of burning the ships, to avoid becoming the slaves of their captors' wives."

There are more stories and eyewitness accounts of giant people and bones being found on the island of Crete, than anywhere in the world as this information is current. In addition to the eyewitness accounts and bones that have been found here that help verify this history with some science, there is more scientific evidence in the form of the tools that these giant people had used. Tools such as the massive double headed axes that have been found in Crete. These axes are said to be from up to 1700 years before Christ and were also the main religious symbol of the ancient Cretans. They date to the Second Palace and Post-Palace periods (1700 - 1300 BC)". The Minoan name for the double axe is "labrys", thus the word labyrinth may originally have meant the "House of the Double Axe," an ancient reference to the invention of the double axe which is attributed to giants.

This biblical story may give us a clue as to what eventually had happened to these giants from Crete:

The sons of Joseph were authorized to invade the "Land of the Giants" and **Og**, the king of Bashan, and the last sovereign of the Ashtoreth dynasty, encountered Moses at Edrei, where he fell "with his sons, and all his people, until there was none left alive, and they (the Israelites) possessed the land," Numbers. xxi. 33, 34, 35.

Deuteronomy 2:11 Which also **were accounted giants**, as the Anakims; but the Moabites call them Emims.

Deuteronomy 3:13 And the rest of Gilead, and all Bashan, being the kingdom of **Og**, gave I unto the half tribe of Manasseh; all the region of Argob, with all Bashan, **which was called the land of giants**.

Joshua 12:4 And the coast of **Og king of Bashan, which was of the remnant of the giants**, that dwelt at Ashtaroth and at Edrei,

Joshua 13:12 All the kingdom of Og in Bashan, which reigned in Ashtaroth and in Edrei, **who remained of the remnant of the giants: for these did Moses smite, and cast them out**.

Fossilized human footprints have also been discovered in Sweden, and in Mexico. Giant skeletons have been discovered throughout the United States and giant fossilized remains are not solely exclusive to the lands of Crete but rather world-wide. Photos of giants from recent times are all a part of important natural history. An article from Strand magazine (December,1895) reprinted in "Traces of the Elder Faiths" of Ireland by W.G. Wood-Martin mentions this fossilized giant discovered during mining operations in County Antrim, Ireland:

"Pre-eminent among the most extraordinary articles ever held by a railway company is the fossilized Irish giant, which is at this moment lying at the London and North-Western Railway Company's Broad street goods depot, and a photograph of which is reproduced here. . . This monstrous figure is reputed to have been dug up by a Mr. Dyer whilst prospecting for iron ore in County Antrim. The principal measurements are: entire length, 12ft. 2in.; girth of chest, 6ft. 6in.; and length of arms, 4ft. 6in. There are six toes on the right foot. The gross weight is 2 tons; 15cwt.; so that it took half a dozen men and a powerful crane to place this article of lost property in position for the Strand magazine photographer to do her work."

The below is the picture of the Irish giant published in Strand Magazine 1895:

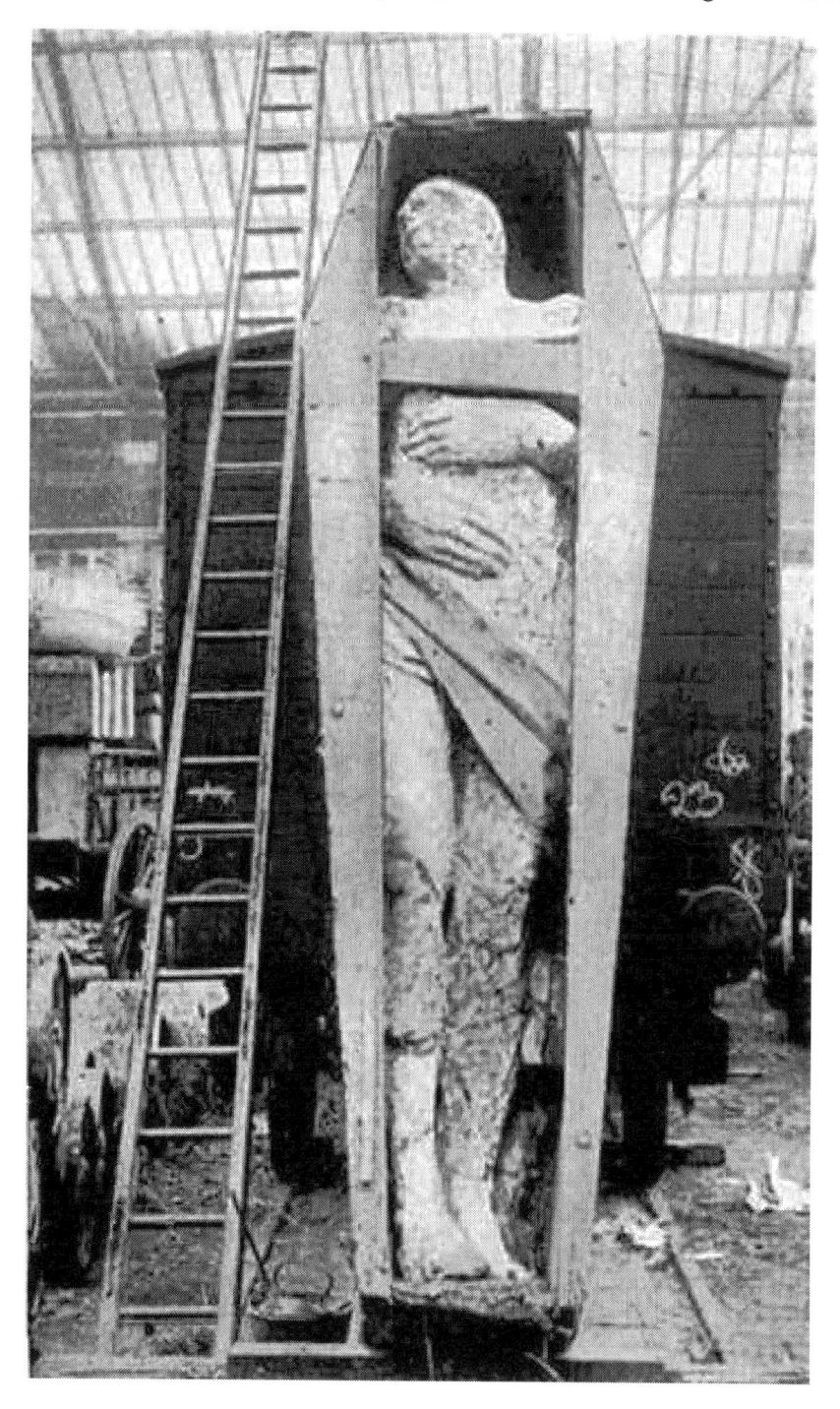

Near Crittenden, Arizona, in 1891, workmen excavating for a commercial building came upon a huge stone sarcophagus eight feet below the surface. The contractor called in expert help, and the sarcophagus was opened to reveal a granite mummy case which had once held the body of a human being more than twelve feet tall - a human with six toes, according to the carving of the case. But the body had been buried so many thousands of years that it had long since turned to dust. Just another silent witness to the truth of Genesis, which tells us that there were giants on the earth in those days, **the excavation of over a dozen skeletons 8 to 12 feet tall, around the world** shocked archaeologists.

If you have already read through the Book of Giants then you may understand why on so many Sumerian artifacts that we find depictions of giant humans being served by lesser humans in stature. As the Book of Enoch testifies, and as other texts of the same body of knowledge tell us, some men worshipped these giants only to have them eventually turn on them.

". . . they took and imprisoned all the helpers that were in the heavens. And the angels themselves descended from the heaven to the earth. And (when) the two hundred demons saw those angels, they were much afraid and worried. They assumed the shape of men and hid themselves. Thereupon the angels forcibly removed the men from the demons, (10) laid them aside, and put watchers over them. . . . the giants . . . . were sons . . . with each other in bodily union . . . . with each other self- . . . . and the . . . . that had been born to them, they forcibly removed them from the demons. And they led one half of them (20) eastwards, and the other half westwards, on the skirts of four huge mountains, towards the foot of the Sumeru mountain, into thirty-two towns which the Living Spirit had prepared for them in the beginning. And one calls (that place) Aryn-waižan. And those men are (>or: were) . . . . in the first arts and crafts. (30) . . . . they made . . . the angels . . . and to the demons . . they went to fight. And those two hundred demons fought a hard battle with the four angels, until the angels used fire, naphtha, and brimstone. . ." - Book of Giants - Sogdian Manuscript

Of such cities mentioned in the Book of Giants other authorities on the antiquities of history make note:

Cristoforo Buondelmonti (1386-1430) was an Italian monk, traveler, and a pioneer in promoting first-hand knowledge of Greece and its antiquities, who had written about a Cretan city named Sarandopolis that was formerly inhabited by giants, and where modern eparkhia of Setia derived its name. This is just one absolutely verifiable instance out of an array of others.

The San Diego Giant

The mummy remains of a giant were unearthed in a cave near San Diego, California. It was discovered by a party of prospectors, and was displayed at the Atlantic exposition while, a number of Smithsonian scientists were there. They asked permission to examine it and when consent was given applied their tapes and found that it measured eight feet four inches from crown to heel. The body lied rest in a ten foot coffin. The exhibitor agreed to sell it for $500 to the Smithsonian of which sold it in more recent days to an "unknown private collector." The following photo is the San Diego Giant:

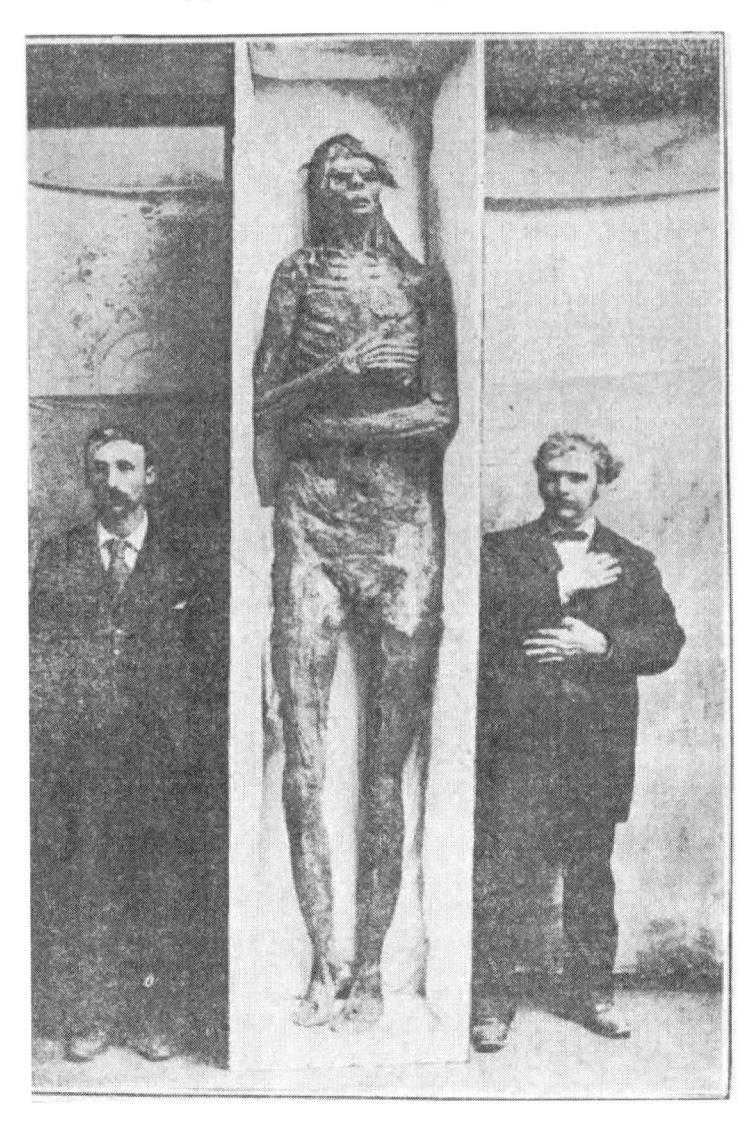

In terms of the **life spans** of the giants we find that it was appointed to them **500 years to live**:

Enoch 4:12 And to Gabriel said the Lord, "Proceed against the bastards and the reprobates, and against the children of fornication and destroy the children of the Watchers from amongst men. Send them one against the other that they may destroy each other in battle, for length of days shall they not have. And no request that they make of thee shall be granted unto their fathers on their behalf; for they hope to live an eternal life, **and that each one of them will live five hundred years**." - Enoch Book 1: Watchers Ch.4:12

Notice how that is specific to a definite degree? Well it would seem that their days were numbered as a curse and that perhaps they couldn't die until 500 years had been allotted to them. Keep in mind that God was not pleased at all with that the fallen angels had done and was using this as a testament against them for breaking His laws. They wanted their giant sons to have the eternal life like they had but God denied their plea for this. Although the exact contents of the petition the fallen angels had Enoch deliver to God is not known this verse appears to be a logical response to one of the things the fallen must have included in it regarding their sons length of life.

Furthermore, in regards to their hybrid status (half man, half angel) of existence we are encountered with the terms and conditions of their afterlife as the Book of the Words of Righteousness tells us:

Enoch 5:28 And now, the giants, who are produced from the spirits and flesh, shall be called evil spirits upon the earth, and on the earth shall be their dwelling.

Enoch 5:29 Evil spirits have proceeded from their bodies; because they are born from men and from the Watchers is their beginning and primal origin; they shall be evil spirits on earth, and evil spirits shall they be called.

Enoch 5:30 And the spirits of the giants afflict, oppress, destroy, attack, do battle, and work destruction on the earth, and cause trouble. They take no food, but nevertheless hunger and thirst, and cause offences.

Not having souls, once the giants had died they became roaming spirits of the earth. Being able to inhabit the bodies of men and women, animals, and other "forms." Only when reading through the Testament of Solomon do we find evidence of these evil spirits residing on earth until the final judgement.

Solomon 1:70. And there came before my face another enslaved spirit, having obscurely the form of a man, with gleaming eyes, and bearing in his hand a blade. And I asked: "Who art thou?" But he answered: "I am a *lascivious spirit*, engendered of a giant man who died in the massacre in the time of the giants." I said to him: "Tell me what thou art employed upon earth, and where thou hast thy dwelling."

Closing notes and my own personal observations:

Being a former evolutionist (macro), finding about OOPARTS and fossilized giant human beings around the world compelled me to look for answers outside the modern scientific religion and into the accounts of historians, scribes, and the body of knowledge of the divine. The earth and its artifacts seem to testify to its own past so long as we pay attention to the ancient reporters who so diligently made the happenings of ancient times known to us through the preservation of their observations. The more one goes looking for evidence pertaining to giants, the more one finds. The bulk of information pertaining to these giants seems to be clustered on the body of biblical knowledge of which no other codex contains more references or information about. This mystery itself seems best solved by pouring over the evidence with diligent study performed by reading with not the eyes but rather the heart.

External References to Enoch

Genesis 4:17 And Cain knew his wife; and she conceived, and bare Enoch: and he builded a city, and called the name of the city, after the name of his son, Enoch.

Genesis 4:18 And unto Enoch was born Irad: and Irad begat Mehujael: and Mehujael begat Methusael: and Methusael begat Lamech.

Genesis 5:18 And Jared lived an hundred sixty and two years, and he begat Enoch:

Genesis 5:19 And Jared lived after he begat Enoch eight hundred years, and begat sons and daughters:

Genesis 5:21 And Enoch lived sixty and five years, and begat Methuselah:

Genesis 5:22 And Enoch walked with God after he begat Methuselah three hundred years, and begat sons and daughters:

Genesis 5:23 And all the days of Enoch were three hundred sixty and five years:

Genesis 5:24 And Enoch walked with God: and he was not; **for God took him.**

Luke 3:37 Which was the son of Mathusala, which was the son of Enoch, which was the son of Jared, which was the son of Maleleel, which was the son of Cainan,

Hebrews 11:5 By faith Enoch was translated that he should not see death; and was not found, because God had translated him: for before his translation he had this testimony, that he pleased God.

Jude 1:14 And Enoch also, the seventh from Adam, prophesied of these, saying, Behold, the Lord cometh with ten thousands of his saints,

COMPARE THESE 4 VERSES

Hebrews 11:5 By *faith* Enoch was translated that he should not see death; and was not found, because God had translated him: for before his translation he had this testimony, that he pleased God.

Hebrews 11:6 But *without faith it is impossible* to please him: for he that cometh to God must believe that he is, and that he is a rewarder of them that diligently seek him.

Enoch 4:5 And it came to pass after this that my spirit was translated and it ascended into the heavens I saw the holy sons of God.

Enoch 4:10 And he translated my spirit into the heaven of heavens and I saw there as it were a structure built of crystals and between those crystals tongues of living fire.

BOOK OF JUBILEES

Jubilees 1:15 And in the second week of the tenth jubilee of Maleleel took unto him a wife Dinah, the daughter of Barakel, the daughter of his brother's brother and she bore him a son in the sixth year and he called his name Jared **for in his days the angels of the Lord descended on the earth**, those so named the Watchers. - *(This verse seems to foreshadow the life and times of Enoch considering Jared was his earthly father.)*

Jubilees 1:22 And he testified to the Watchers, who had sinned with the daughters of men; for these had begun to unite themselves, so as to be defiled, with the daughters of men, and **Enoch testified against them all**.

Jubilees 10:17 And in his life on earth he excelled the children of men save Enoch because of the righteousness, wherein he was perfect. For **Enoch's office was ordained for a testimony to the generations of the world, so that he should recount all the deeds of generation unto generation, till the Day of Judgment.**

Jubilees 19:24 And in his seed shall my name be blessed, and the name of my fathers, Shem, and Noab, and **Enoch**, and Mahalalel, and Enos, and Seth, and Adam.

Jubilees 19:25 And these shall serve to lay the foundations of the heaven, and to strengthen the earth, and to renew all the luminaries which are in the firmament.

Jubilees 19:27 Jacob, my beloved son, whom my soul loves, may YAHWEH bless you from above the firmament, and may He give you all the blessings wherewith He blessed Adam, and **Enoch**, and Noah, and Shem; and all the things of which He told me, and all the things which He promised to give me, may he cause to cleave to you and to your seed forever, according to the days of heaven above the earth.

Jubilees 21:10 And eat its meat on that day and on the second day, and let not the sun on the second day go down upon it till it is eaten, and let nothing be left over for the third day; for it is not acceptable and let it no longer be eaten, and all who eat thereof will bring sin upon themselves; for thus I have found it written in the books of my forefathers, **and in the words of Enoch**, and in the words of Noah.

Jubilees 38:8 And Simeon and Benjamin and **Enoch, Reuben's son**, went forth on the west side of the tower, and **fifty** men with them, and they slew of Edom and of the Horites four hundred men, stout warriors; and six hundred fled, and four of the sons of Esau fled with them, and left their father lying slain, as he had fallen on the hill which is in 'Aduram. (*This Scripture is a spiritual symbolism of Elijah another righteous man whom God took up who will be witnesses to the whole world Revelations 11. Adding to this and what makes one draw this spiritual insight is that this verse **is not talking about the same Enoch who wrote the Book of Enoch but rather Ruben's son.** If you make note of the same name use you may find that important when considering the Elijah and Elisha paradox...*)

ENOCH & ELIJAH IN REVELATIONS

Although Enoch is not mentioned directly by name, nor is Elijah, these are the only two biblical characters who never died. The Bible is very specific in regarding its records of people dying. It makes mention of when these biblical patriarchs die over and over again. Going out of its way to record them and yet there is no record of Enoch or Elijah dying anywhere in the whole of the body of biblical knowledge. So, then we have in the last book of the Bible, Revelation at chapter 11 the appearance of two prophets wearing sack cloth. Biblical scholars and myself included believe these two men to be none other than Enoch and Elijah. What they do in Revelations fits with the lives they lived completely. See for yourself and test the Scriptures to find out if it's Enoch and Elijah… The following is the chapter in question. Keep in mind, this happens in the future.

Revelation 11 - King James Version (KJV)

[1] And there was given me a reed like unto a rod: and the angel stood, saying, Rise, and measure the temple of God, and the altar, and them that worship therein.

[2] But the court which is without the temple leave out, and measure it not; for it is given unto the Gentiles: and the holy city shall they tread under foot forty and two months.

[3] And I will give power unto my two witnesses, and they shall prophesy a thousand two hundred and threescore days, clothed in sackcloth.

[4] These are the two olive trees, and the two candlesticks standing before the God of the earth.

[5] And if any man will hurt them, fire proceedeth out of their mouth, and devoureth their enemies: and if any man will hurt them, he must in this manner be killed.

[6] These have power to shut heaven, that it rain not in the days of their prophecy: and have power over waters to turn them to blood, and to smite the earth with all plagues, as often as they will.

⁷ And when they shall have finished their testimony, the beast that ascendeth out of the bottomless pit shall make war against them, and shall overcome them, and kill them.

⁸ And their dead bodies shall lie in the street of the great city, which spiritually is called Sodom and Egypt, where also our Lord was crucified.

⁹ And they of the people and kindreds and tongues and nations shall see their dead bodies three days and an half, and shall not suffer their dead bodies to be put in graves.

¹⁰ And they that dwell upon the earth shall rejoice over them, and make merry, and shall send gifts one to another; because these two prophets tormented them that dwelt on the earth.

¹¹ And after three days and an half the spirit of life from God entered into them, and they stood upon their feet; and great fear fell upon them which saw them.

¹² And they heard a great voice from heaven saying unto them, Come up hither. And they ascended up to heaven in a cloud; and their enemies beheld them.

¹³ And the same hour was there a great earthquake, and the tenth part of the city fell, and in the earthquake were slain of men seven thousand: and the remnant were affrighted, and gave glory to the God of heaven.

¹⁴ The second woe is past; and, behold, the third woe cometh quickly.

¹⁵ And the seventh angel sounded; and there were great voices in heaven, saying, The kingdoms of this world are become the kingdoms of our Lord, and of his Christ; and he shall reign for ever and ever.

¹⁶ And the four and twenty elders, which sat before God on their seats, fell upon their faces, and worshipped God,

¹⁷ Saying, We give thee thanks, O LORD God Almighty, which art, and wast, and art to come; because thou hast taken to thee thy great power, and hast reigned.

[18] And the nations were angry, and thy wrath is come, and the time of the dead, that they should be judged, and that thou shouldest give reward unto thy servants the prophets, and to the saints, and them that fear thy name, small and great; and shouldest destroy them which destroy the earth.

[19] And the temple of God was opened in heaven, and there was seen in his temple the ark of his testament: and there were lightnings, and voices, and thunderings, and an earthquake, and great hail.

TESTAMENT OF SOLOMON

1. Testament of Solomon, son of David, who was king in Jerusalem, and mastered and controlled all spirits of the air, on the earth, and under the earth. By means of them also he wrought all the transcendent works of the Temple. Telling also of the authorities they wield against men, and by what angels these demons are brought to naught.

Of the sage Solomon.

Blessed art thou, O Lord God, who didst give Solomon such authority. Glory to thee and might unto the ages. Amen.

2. And behold, when the Temple of the city of Jerusalem was being built, and the artificers were working thereat, Ornias the demon came among them toward sunset; and he took away half of the pay of the master workman's little boy, as well as half his food. He also continued to suck the thumb of his right hand every day. And the child grew thin, although he was very much loved by the king.

3. So King Solomon called the boy one day, and questioned him, saying: "Do I not love thee more than all the artisans who are working in the Temple of God? Do I not give thee double wages and a double supply of food? How is it that day by day and hour by hour thou growest thinner?"

4. But the child said to the king: "I pray thee, O king. Listen to what has befallen all that thy child hath. After we are all released from our work on the Temple of God, after sunset, when I lie down to rest, one of the evil demons comes and takes away from me one half of my pay and one half of my food. Then he also takes hold of my right hand and sucks my thumb. And lo, my soul is oppressed, and so my body waxes thinner every day."

5. Now when I Solomon heard this, I entered the Temple of God, and prayed with all my soul, night and day, that the demon might be delivered into my hands, and that I might gain authority over him. And it came about through my prayer that grace was given to me from the Lord Sabaoth by Michael his archangel. He brought me a little ring, having a seal consisting of an engraved stone, and said to me: "Take, O Solomon, king, son of David, the gift which the Lord God has sent thee, the highest Sabaoth. With it thou shalt lock up all demons of the earth, male and female; and with their help thou shalt build up Jerusalem. But thou must wear this seal of God. And this engraving of the seal of the ring sent thee is a Pentalpha."

(A Pentalpha otherwise known as the seal of Solomon.)

6. And I Solomon was overjoyed, and praised and glorified the God of heaven and earth. And on the morrow I called the boy, and gave him the ring, and said to him: "take this, and at the hour in which the demon shall come unto thee, throw this ring at the chest of the demon, and say to him: 'In the name of God, King Solomon calls thee hither. And then do thou come running to me, without having any misgivings or fear in respect of aught thou mayest hear on the part of the demon."

7. So the child took the ring, and went off; and behold, at the customary hour Ornias, the fierce demon, came like a burning fire to take the pay from the child. But the child according to the instructions received from the king, threw the ring at the chest of the demon, and said: "King Solomon calls thee hither." And then he went off at a run to the king. But the demon cried out aloud, saying: "Child, why hast thou done this to me? Take the ring off me, and I will render to thee the gold of the earth. Only take this off me, and forbear to lead me away to Solomon."

8. But the child said to the demon: "As the Lord God of Israel liveth, I will not brook thee. So come hither." And the child came at a run, rejoicing, to the king, and said: "I have brought the demon, O king, as thou didst command me, O my master. And behold, he stands before the gates of the court of thy palace, crying out, and supplicating with a loud voice; offering me the silver and gold of the earth if I will only bring him unto thee."

9. And when Solomon heard this, he rose up from his throne, and went outside into the vestibule of the court of his palace; and there he saw the demon, shuddering and trembling. And he said to him: "Who art thou?" And the demon answered: "I am called Ornias."

10. And Solomon said to him: "Tell me, O demon, to what zodiacal sign thou art subject." And he answered: "To the Water-pourer. And those who are consumed with desire for the noble virgins upon earth, these I strangle. But in case there is no disposition to sleep, I am changed into three forms. Whenever men come to be enamoured of women, I metamorphose myself into a comely female; and I take

hold of the men in their sleep, and play with them. And after a while I again take to my wings, and hie me to the heavenly regions. I also appear as a lion, and I am commanded by all the demons. I am frustrated by the archangel Uriel, the power of God."

11. I Solomon, having heard the name of the archangel, prayed and glorified God, the Lord of heaven and earth. And I sealed the demon and set him to work at stone-cutting, so that he might cut the stones in the Temple, which, lying along the shore, had been brought by the Sea of Arabia. But he, fearful of the iron, continued and said to me: "I pray thee, King Solomon, let me go free; and I will bring you all the demons." And as he was not willing to be subject to me, I prayed the archangel Uriel to come and succour me; and I forthwith beheld the archangel Uriel coming down to me from the heavens.

12. And the angel bade the whales of the sea come out of the abyss. And he cast his destiny upon the ground, and that destiny made subject to him the great demon. And he commanded the great demon and bold Ornias, to cut stones at the Temple. And accordingly I Solomon glorified the God of heaven and Maker of the earth. And he bade Ornias come with his destiny, and gave him the seal, saying: "Away with thee, and bring me hither the prince of all the demons."

13. So Ornias took the finger-ring, and went off to Beelzeboul, who has kingship over the demons. He said to him: "Hither! Solomon calls thee." But Beelzeboul, having heard, said to him: "Tell me, who is this Solomon of whom thou speakest to me?" Then Ornias threw the ring at the chest of Beelzeboul, saying: "Solomon the king calls thee." But Beelzeboul cried aloud with a mighty voice, and shot out a great burning flame of fire; and he arose, and followed Ornias, and came to Solomon.

14. And when I saw the prince of demons, I glorified the Lord God, Maker of heaven and earth, and I said: "Blessed art thou, Lord God Almighty, who hast given to Solomon thy servant wisdom, the assessor of the wise, and hast subjected unto me all the power of the devils."

15. And I questioned him, and said: "Who art thou?" The demon replied: "I am Beelzebub, the exarch of the demons. And all the demons have their chief seats close to me. And I it is who make manifest the apparition of each demon." And he promised to bring to me in bonds all the unclean spirits. And I again glorified the God of heaven and earth, as I do always give thanks to him.

16. I then asked of the demon if there were females among them. And when he told me that there were, I said that I desired to see them. So Beelzeboul went off

at high speed, and brought unto me Onoskelis, that had a very pretty shape, and the skin of a fairhued woman; and she tossed her head.

17. And when she was come, I said to her: "Tell me who art thou?" But she said to me: "I am called Onoskelis, a spirit which has been made into a body, lurking upon the earth. There is a golden cave where I lie. But I have a place that ever shifts. At one time I strangle men with a noose; at another, I creep up and prevent them from their true natures. But my most frequent dwelling-places are the precipices, caves, and ravines. Oftentimes, however, do I consort with men in the semblance of a woman, and above all with those of a dark skin. For they share my star with me; since they it is who privily or openly worship my star, without knowing that they harm themselves, and but whet my appetite for further mischief. For they wish to provide money by means of remembering me, but I supply a little to those who worship me fairly."

18. And I Solomon questioned her about her birth, and she replied: "I was born of a voice untimely, the so-called echo of a man's ordure dropped in a wood."

19. And I said to her: "Under what star dost thou pass?" And she answered me: "Under the star of the full moon, for the reason that the moon travels over most things." Then I said to her: "And what angel is it that frustrates thee?" And she said to me: "He that in thee is reigning." And I thought that she mocked me, and bade a soldier strike her. But she cried aloud, and said: "I am subjected to thee, O king, by the wisdom of God given to thee, and by the angel Joel."

20. So I commanded her to spin the hemp for the ropes used in the building of the house of God; and accordingly, when I had sealed and bound her, she was so overcome and brought to naught as to stand night and day spinning the hemp.

21. And I at once bade another demon to be led unto me; and instantly there approached me the demon Asmodeus, bound, and I asked him: "Who art thou?" But he shot on me a glance of anger and rage, and said: "And who art thou?" And I said to him: "Thus punished as thou art, answerest thou me not?" But he, with rage, said to me: "But how shall I answer thee, for thou art a son of man; whereas I was born of an angel's seed by a daughter of man, so that no word of our heavenly kind addressed to the earth-born can be overweening. Wherefore also my star is bright in heaven, and men call it, some the Wain, and some the dragon's child. I keep near unto this star. So ask me not many things; for thy kingdom also after a little time is to be disrupted, and thy glory is but for a season. And short will be thy tyranny over us; and then we shall again have free range over mankind, so as that they shall revere us as if we were gods, not knowing, men that they are, the names of the angels set over us."

22. And I Solomon, on hearing this, bound him more carefully, and ordered him to be flogged with thongs of ox-hide, and to tell me humbly what was his name and of his business. And he answered me thus: "I am called Asmodeus among mortals, and my business is to plot against the newly wedded, so that they may not know one another. And I sever them utterly by many calamities, and I waste away the beauty of virgin women, and estrange their hearts."

23. And I said to him: "Is this thy only business?" And he answered me: "I transport men into fits of madness and desire, when they have wives of their own, so that they leave them, and go off by night and day to others that belong to other men; with the result that they commit sin, and fall into murderous deeds."

24. And I adjured him by the name of the Lord Sabaôth, saying: "Fear God, Asmodeus, and tell me by what angel thou art frustrated." But he said: "By Raphael, the archangel that stands before the throne of God. But the liver and gall of a fish put me to flight, when smoked over ashes of the tamarisk." I again asked him, and said: "Hide not aught from me. For I am Solomon, son of David, King of Israel. Tell me the name of the fish which thou reverest." And he answered: "It is the glanos by name, and is found in the rivers of Assyria; wherefore it is that I roam about in those parts."

25. And I said to him: "Hast thou nothing else about thee, Asmodeus?" And he answered: "The power of God knoweth, which hath bound me with the indissoluble bonds of yonder one's seal, that whatever I have told thee is true. I pray thee, King Solomon, condemn me not to go into water." But I smiled, and said to him: "As the Lord God of my fathers liveth, I will lay iron on thee to wear. But thou shalt also make the clay for the entire construction of the Temple, treading it down with thy feet." And I ordered them to give him ten water jars to carry water in. And the demon groaned terribly, and did the work I ordered him to do. And this I did, because that fierce demon Asmodeus knew even the future. And I Solomon glorified God, who gave wisdom to me Solomon his servant. And the liver of the fish and its gall I hung on the spike of a reed, and burned it over Asmodeus because of his being so strong, and his unbearable malice was thus frustrated.

26. And I summoned again to stand before me Beelzeboul, the prince of demons, and I sat him down on a raised seat of honour, and said to him: "Why art thou alone, prince of the demons?" And he said to me: "Because I alone am left of the angels of heaven that came down. For I was first angel in the first heaven being entitled Beelzeboul. And now I control all those who are bound in Tartarus. But I too have a child, and he haunts the Red Sea. And on any suitable occasion he comes up to me again, being subject to me; and reveals to me what he has done, and when he is ready, he will come in triumph.

27. I Solomon said unto him: "Beelzeboul, what is thy employment?" And he answered me: "I destroy kings. I bring destruction by means of tyrants. And my own demons I send on to men to be worshipped, in order that the latter may believe in them and be lost. And the chosen servants of God, priests and faithful men, I excite unto desires for wicked sins, and evil heresies, and lawless deeds; and they obey me, and I bear them on to destruction. And I inspire men with envy, and desire for murder, and for wars and sodomy, and other evil things. I bring about jealousies and murders in a country, and I instigate wars. I will destroy the world."

28. So I said to him: "Bring to me thy child, who is, as thou sayest, in the Red Sea." But he said to me: "I will not bring him to thee. But there shall come to me another demon called Ephippas. Him will I bind, and he will bring him up from the deep unto me." And I said to him: "How comes thy son to be in the depth of the sea, and what is his name? "And he answered me: "Ask me not, for thou canst not learn from me. However, he will come to thee by any command, and will tell thee openly." So I said to him: "Tell me in which star you reside." To which he answered, "The one called by men the Evening Star."

29. I said to him: "Tell me by what angel thou art frustrated." And he answered: "By the holy and precious name of the Almighty God, called by the Hebrews by a row of numbers, of which the sum is 644, and among the Greeks it is Emmanuel. And if one of the Romans adjure me by the great name of the power Eleéth, I disappear at once."

30. I Solomon was astounded when I heard this; and I ordered him to saw up Theban marbles. And when he began to saw the marbles, the other demons cried out with a loud voice, howling because of their king Beelzeboul was also subject to the power the Most High had given me over him.

31. But I Solomon questioned him, saying: "If thou wouldst gain a respite, discourse to me about the things in heaven." And Beelzeboul said: "Hear, O king, if thou burn gum, and incense, and bulb of the seal, with nard and saffron, and light seven lamps in an earthquake, thou wilt firmly fix thy house. And if, being pure, thou light them at dawn in the sun alight, then wilt thou see the heavenly dragons, how they wind themselves along and drag the chariot of the sun."

32. And I Solomon, having heard this, rebuked him, and said: "Silence for this present time, and continue to saw the marbles as I commanded thee." And I Solomon praised God, and commanded another demon to present himself to me. And one came before me who carried his face high up in the air, but the rest of the spirit curled away like a snail. And it broke through the few soldiers, and raised also a terrible dust on the ground, and carried it upwards; and then again

hurled it back to frighten us, and asked what questions I could ask as a rule. And I stood up, and spat on the ground in that spot, and sealed the demon with the ring of God. And forthwith the dustwind stopped. Then I asked him, saying: "Who art thou, O wind?" Then he once more shook up a dust, and answered me: "What wouldst thou have, King Solomon?" I answered him: "Tell me what thou art called, and I would fain ask thee a question. But so far I give thanks to God who has made me wise to answer your evil plots."

33. But [the demon] answered me: "I am the spirit of the ashes (Tephras)." And I said to him: "What is thy pursuit?" And he said: "I bring darkness on men, and set fire to fields; and I bring homesteads to naught. But most busy am I in summer. However, when I get an opportunity, I creep into corners of the wall, by night and day. For I am offspring of the great one, and nothing less." Accordingly I said to him: "Under what star dost thou lie?" And he answered: "In the very tip of the moon's horn, when it is found in the south. There is my star. For I have been bidden to restrain the convulsions of the hemitertian fever; and this is why many men pray to the hemitertian fever, using these three names: Bultala, Thallal, Melchal. And I heal them." And I said to him: "I am Solomon; when therefore thou wouldst do harm, by whose aid dost thou do it?" But he said to me: "By the angel's, by whom also the third day's fever is lulled to rest." So I questioned him, and said: "And by what name?" And he answered: "That of the archangel Azael." And I summoned the archangel Azael, and set a seal on the demon, and commanded him to seize great stones, and toss them up to the workmen on the higher parts of the Temple. And, being compelled, the demon began to do what he was bidden to do.

34. And I glorified God afresh who gave me this authority, and ordered another demon to come before me. And there came seven spirits, females, bound and woven together, fair in appearance and comely. And I Solomon, seeing them, questioned them and said: "Who are ye?" But they, with one accord, said with one voice: "We are of the thirty-three elements of the cosmic ruler of the darkness." And the first said: "I am Deception." The second said: "I am Strife." The third: "I am Klothod, which is battle." The fourth: "I am Jealousy." The fifth: "I am Power." The sixth: "I am Error." The seventh: "I am the worst of all, and our stars are in heaven. Seven stars humble in sheen, and all together. And we are called as it were Goddesses. We change our place all and together, and together we live, sometimes in Lydia, sometimes in Olympus, sometimes in a great mountain."

35. So I Solomon questioned them one by one, beginning with the first, and going down to the seventh. The first said: "I am Deception, I deceive and weave snares here and there. I whet and excite heresies. But I have an angel who frustrates me, Lamechalal."

36. Likewise also the second said: "I am Strife, strife of strifes. I bring timbers, stones, hangers, my weapons on the spot. But I have an angel who frustrates me, Baruchiachel."

37. Likewise also the third said: "I am called Klothod, which is Battle, and I cause the well behaved to scatter and fall foul one of the other. And why do I say so much? I have an angel that frustrates me: "Marmarath.""

38. Likewise also the fourth said: "I cause men to forget their sobriety and moderation. I part them and split them into parties; for Strife follows me hand in hand. I rend the husband from the sharer of his bed, and children from parents, and brothers from sisters. But why tell so much to my despite? I have an angel that frustrates me, the great Balthial."

39. Likewise also the fifth said: "I am Power. By power I raise up tyrants and tear down kings. To all rebels I furnish power. I have an angel that frustrates me, Asteraôth."

40. Likewise also the sixth said: "I am Error, O King Solomon. And I will make thee to err, as I have before made thee to err, when I caused thee to slay thy own brother. I will lead you into error, so as to pry into graves; and I teach them that dig, and I lead errant souls away from all piety, and many other evil traits are mine. But I have an angel that frustrates me, Uriel."

41. Likewise also the seventh said: "I am the worst, and I make thee worse off than thou wast; because I will impose the bonds of Artemis. But the locust will set me free, for by means thereof is it fated that thou shalt achieve my desire. For if one were wise, he would not turn his steps toward me."

42. So I Solomon, having heard and wondered, sealed them with my ring; and since they were so considerable, I bade them dig the foundations of the Temple of God. For the length of it was 250 cubits. And I bade them be industrious, and with one murmur of joint protest they began to perform the tasks enjoined.

43. But I Solomon glorified the Lord, and bade another demon come before me. And there was brought to me a demon having all the limbs of a man, but without a head. And I, seeing him, said to him: "Tell me, who art thou?" And he answered: "I am a demon." So I said to him: "Which?" And he answered me: "I am called Envy. For I delight to devour heads, being desirous to secure for myself a head; but I do not eat enough, but am anxious to have such a head as thou hast."

44. I Solomon, on hearing this, sealed him, stretching out my hand against his chest. Whereon the demon leapt up, and threw himself down, and gave a groan, saying: "Woe is me! Where am I come to? O traitor Ornias, I cannot see!" So I said to him: "I am Solomon. Tell me then how thou dost manage to see!" And he answered me: "By means of my feelings." I then, Solomon, having heard his voice come up to me, asked him how he managed to speak. And he answered me: "I, O King Solomon, am wholly voice, for I have inherited the voices of many men. For in the case of all men who are called dumb, I it is who smashed their heads, when they were children and had reached their eighth day. Then when a child is crying in the night, I become a spirit, and glide by means of his voice. In the crossways also I have many services to render, and my encounter is fraught with harm. For I grasp in all instants a man's head, and with my hands, as with a sword, I cut it off, and put it on to myself. And in this way, by means of the fire which is in me, through my neck it is swallowed up. I it is that sends grave mutilations and incurables on men's feet, and inflict sores."

45. And I Solomon, on hearing this, said to him: "Tell me how thou dost discharge forth the fire? Out of what sources dost thou emit it?" And the spirit said to me: "From the Day-star. For here hath not yet been found that Elburion, to whom men offer prayers and kindle lights. And his name is invoked by the seven demons before me. And he cherishes them."

46. But I said to him: "Tell me his name." But he answered: "I cannot tell thee. For if I tell his name, I render myself incurable. But he will come in response to his name." And on hearing this, I Solomon said to him: "Tell me then, by what angel thou art frustrated?" And he answered: "By the fiery flash of lightning." And I bowed myself before the Lord God of Israel, and bade him remain in the keeping of Beelzeboul until the angel Iax should come.

47. Then I ordered another demon to come before me, and there came into my presence a hound, having a very large shape, and it spoke with a loud voice, and said, "Hail, Lord, King Solomon!" And I Solomon was astounded. I said to it: Who art thou, O hound?" And it answered: "I do indeed seem to thee to be a hound, but before thou wast, O King Solomon, I was a man that wrought many unholy deeds on earth. I was surpassingly learned in letters, and was so mighty that I could hold the stars of heaven back. And many divine works did I prepare. For I do harm to men who follow after our star, and change them to. And I seize the frenzied men by the larynx, and so destroy them."

48. And I Solomon said to him: "What is thy name?" And he answered: "Staff" (Rabdos). And I said to him: "What is thine employment? And what results canst thou achieve?" And he replied: "Give me thy servant, and I will lead him away

into a mountainous spot, and will show him a green stone tossed to and fro, with which thou mayest adorn the temple of the Lord God."

49. And I Solomon, on hearing this, ordered my servant to set off with him, and to take the finger-ring bearing the seal of God with him. And I said to him: "Whoever shall show thee the green stone, seal him with this finger-ring. And mark the spot with care, and bring me the demon hither." And the demon showed him the green stone, and he sealed it, and brought the demon to me. And I Solomon decided to confine with my seal on my right hand the two, the headless demon, likewise the hound, that was so huge; he should be bound as well. And I bade the hound keep safe the fiery spirit so that lamps as it were might by day and night cast their light through its maw on the artisans at work.

50. And I Solomon took from the mine of that stone 200 shekels for the supports of the table of incense, which was similar in appearance. And I Solomon glorified the Lord God, and then closed round the treasure of that stone. And I ordered afresh the demons to cut marble for the construction of the house of God. And I Solomon prayed to the Lord, and asked the hound, saying: "By what angel art thou frustrated?" And the demon replied: "By the great Brieus."

51. And I praised the Lord God of heaven and earth, and bade another demon come forward to me; and there came before me one in the form of a roaring lion. And he stood and answered me saying: "O king, in the form which I have, I am a spirit quite incapable of being perceived. Upon all men who lie prostrate with sickness I leap, coming stealthily along; and I render the man weak, so that his habit of body is enfeebled. But I have also another glory, O king. I cast out demons, and I have legions under my control. And I am capable of being received in my dwelling-places, along with all the demons belonging to the legions under me." But I Solomon, on hearing this, asked him: "What is thy name?" But he answered: "Lion-bearer, Rath in kind." And I said to him: "How art thou to be frustrated along with thy legions? What angel is it that frustrates thee?" And he answered: "If I tell thee the name, I bind not myself alone, but also the legions of demons under me."

52. So I said to him: "I adjure thee in the name of the God Sabaoth, to tell me by what name thou art frustrated along with thy host." And the spirit answered me: "The 'Son of Man,' who is to suffer many things at the hands of men, whose name is the figure 644, which is Emmanuel; he it is who has bound us, and who will then come and plunge us from the steep, under water. He is noised abroad in the three letters which bring him down."

53. And I Solomon, on hearing this, glorified God, and condemned his legion to carry wood from the thicket. And I condemned the lion-shaped one himself to

saw up the wood small with his teeth, for burning in the unquenchable furnace for the Temple of God.

54. And I worshipped the Lord God of Israel, and bade another demon come forward. And there came before me a dragon, three-headed, of fearful hue. And I questioned him: "Who art thou?" And he answered me: "I am a caltrop-like spirit, whose activity in three lies. But I blind children in women's wombs, and twirl their ears round. And I make them deaf and mute. And I have again in my third head means of slipping into the body. And I smite men in the limbless part of the body, and cause them to fall down, and foam, and grind their teeth. But I have my own way of being frustrated. Jerusalem being signified in writing, unto the place called 'of the head." For there is fore-appointed the angel of the great counsel, and now he will openly dwell on the cross. He doth frustrate me, and to him am I subject."

55. "But in the place where thou sittest, O King Solomon, standeth a column in the air, of purple...1 The demon called Ephippas hath brought it up from the Red Sea, from inner Arabia. He it is that shall be shut up in a skin-bottle and brought before thee. But at the entrance of the Temple, which thou hast begun to build, O King Solomon, lies stored much gold, which dig thou up and carry off." And I Solomon sent my servant, and found it to be as the demon told me. And I sealed him with my ring, and praised the Lord God."

56. So I said to him: "What art thou called?" And the demon said: "I am the crest of dragons." And I bade him make bricks in the Temple. He had human hands.

57. And I adored the Lord God of Israel, and bade another demon present himself. And there came before me a spirit in woman's form, that had a head without any limbs, and her hair was dishevelled. And I said to her: "Who art thou?" But she answered: "Nay, who art thou? And why dost thou want to hear concerning me? But, as thou wouldst learn, here I stand bound before thy face. Go then into thy royal storehouses and wash thy hands. Then sit down afresh before thy tribunal, and ask me questions; and thou shalt learn, O king, who I am."

58. And I Solomon did as she enjoined me, and restrained myself because of the wisdom dwelling in me; in order that I might hear of her deeds, and reprehend them, and manifest them to men. And I sat down, and said to the demon: "What art thou?" And she said: "I am called among men Obizuth (This is Lilith self-identifying by one of her many names.); and by night I sleep not, but go my rounds over all the world, and visit women in childbirth. And divining the hour I take my stand; and if I am lucky, I strangle the child. But if not, I retire to another place. For I cannot for a single night retire unsuccessful. For I am a fierce spirit, of myriad names and many shapes. And now hither, now thither I roam. And to

westering parts I go my rounds. But as it now is, though thou hast sealed me round with the ring of God, thou hast done nothing. I am not standing before thee, and thou wilt not be able to command me. For I have no work other than the destruction of children, and the making their ears to be deaf, and the working of evil to their eyes, and the binding their mouths with a bond, and the ruin of their minds, and paining of their bodies."

59. When I Solomon heard this, I marvelled at her appearance, for I beheld all her body to be in darkness. But her glance was altogether bright and greeny, and her hair was tossed wildly like a dragon's; and the whole of her limbs were invisible. And her voice was very clear as it came to me. And I cunningly said: "Tell me by what angel thou art frustrated, O evil spirit?" By she answered me: "By the angel of God called Afarôt, which is interpreted Raphael, by whom I am frustrated now and for all time. His name, if any man know it, and write the same on a woman in childbirth, then I shall not be able to enter her. Of this name the number is 640." And I Solomon having heard this, and having glorified the Lord, ordered her hair to be bound, and that she should be hung up in front of the Temple of God; that all the children of Israel, as they passed, might see it, and glorify the Lord God of Israel, who had given me this authority, with wisdom and power from God, by means of this signet.

60. And I again ordered another demon to come before me. And it came, rolling itself along, one in appearance like to a dragon, but having the face and hands of a man. And all its limbs, except the feet, were those of a dragon; and it had wings on its back. And when I beheld it, I was astonished, and said: "Who art thou, demon, and what art thou called? And whence hast thou come? Tell me."

61. And the spirit answered and said: "This is the first time I have stood before thee, O King Solomon. I am a spirit made into a god among men, but now brought to naught by the ring and wisdom given to thee by God. Now I am the so-called winged dragon, and I chamber not with many women, but only with a few that are of fair shape, which possess the name of Touxylou, of this star. And I pair with them in the guise of a spirit winged in form, copulating with them. And she on whom I have leapt goes heavy with child, and that which is born of her becomes filled with lust. But since such offspring cannot be carried by men, the woman in question breaks wind. Such is my role. Supposed then only that I am satisfied, and all the other demons molested and disturbed by thee will speak the whole truth. But those composed of fire will cause to be burned up by fire the material of the logs which is to be collected by them for the building in the Temple."

62. And as the demon said this, I saw the spirit going forth from his mouth, and it consumed the wood of the frankincense-tree, and burned up all the logs which we

had placed in the Temple of God. And I Solomon saw what the spirit had done, and I marvelled.

63. And, having glorified God, I asked the dragon-shaped demon, and said: "Tell me, by what angel art thou frustrated?" And he answered: "By the great angel which has its seat in the second heaven, which is called in Hebrew, Bazazeth. And I Solomon, having heard this, and having invoked his angel, condemned him to saw up marbles for the building of the Temple of God; and I praised God, and commanded another demon to come before me.

64. And there came before my face another spirit, as it were a woman in the form she had. But on her shoulders she had two other heads with hands. And I asked her, and said: "Tell me, who art thou?" And she said to me: "I am Enêpsigos, who also have a myriad names." And I said her: "By what angel art thou frustrated?" But she said to me: "What seekest, what askest thou? I undergo changes, like the goddess I am called. And I change again, and pass into possession of another shape. And be not desirous therefore to know all that concerns me. But since thou art before me for this much, hearken. I have my abode in the moon, and for that reason I possess three forms. At times I am magically invoked by the wise as Kronos. At other times, in connexion with those who bring me down, I come down and appear in another shape. The measure of the element is inexplicable and indefinable, and not to be frustrated. I then, changing into these three forms, come down and become such as thou seest me; but I am frustrated by the angel Rathanael, who sits in the third heaven. This then is why I speak to thee. Yonder temple cannot contain me."

65. I therefore Solomon prayed to my God, and I invoked the angel of whom Enépsigos spoke to me, and used my seal. And I sealed her with a triple chain, and (placed) beneath her the fastening of the chain. I used the seal of God, and the spirit prophesied to me, saying: "This is what thou, King Solomon, doest to us. But after a time thy kingdom shall be broken, and again in season this Temple shall be driven asunder; and all Jerusalem shall be undone by the King of the Persians and Medes and Chaldaeans. And the vessels of this Temple, which thou makest, shall be put to servile uses of the gods; and along with them all the jars, in which thou dost shut us up, shall be broken by the hands of men. And then we shall go forth in great power hither and thither, and be disseminated all over the world. And we shall lead astray the inhabited world for a long season, until the Son of God is stretched upon the cross. For never before doth arise a king like unto him, one frustrating us all, whose mother shall not have contact with man. Who else can receive such authority over spirits, except he, whom the first devil will seek to tempt, but will not prevail over? The number of his name is 644, which is Emmanuel. Wherefore, O King Solomon, thy time is evil, and thy years short and evil, and to thy servant shall thy kingdom be given."

66. And I Solomon, having heard this, glorified God. And though I marvelled at the prophecy of the demon, I did not credit it until it came true. And I did not believe their words; but when they were realized, then I understood, and at my death I wrote this Testament to the children of Israel, and gave it to them, so that they might know the powers of the demons and their shapes, and the names of their angels, by which these angels are frustrated. And I glorified the Lord God of Israel, and commanded the spirits to be bound with bonds indissoluble.

67. And having praised God, I commanded another spirit to come before me; and there came before my face another demon, having in front the shape of a horse, but the behind of a fish. And he had a mighty voice, and said to me: "O King Solomon, I am a fierce spirit of the sea, and I am greedy of gold and silver. I am such a spirit as rounds itself and comes over the expanses of the water of the sea, and I trip up the men who sail thereon. For I round myself into a wave, and transform myself, and then throw myself on ships and come right in on them. And that is my business, and my way of getting hold of money and men. For I take the men, and whirl them round with myself, and hurl the men out of the sea. For I am not covetous of men's bodies, but cast them up out of the sea so far. But since Beelzeboul, ruler of the spirits of air and of those under the earth, and lord of earthly ones, hath a joint kingship with us in respect of the deeds of each one of us, therefore I went up from the sea, to get a certain outlook in his company.

68. "But I also have another character and role. I metamorphose myself into waves, and come up from the sea. And I show myself to men, so that those on earth call me Cynospaston, because I assume the human form. And my name is a true one. For by my passage up into men, I send forth a certain nausea. I came then to take counsel with the prince Beelzeboul; and he bound me and delivered me into thy hands. And I am here before thee because of this seal, and thou dost now torment me. Behold now, in two or three days the spirit that converseth with thee will fail, because I shall have no water."

69. And I said to him: "Tell me by what angel thou art frustrated." And he answered: "By Iameth." And I glorified God. I commanded the spirit to be thrown into a phial along with ten jugs of sea-water of two measures each. And I sealed them round above the marbles and asphalt and pitch in the mouth of the vessel. And having sealed it with my ring, I ordered it to be deposited in the Temple of God. And I ordered another spirit to come before me.

70. And there came before my face another enslaved spirit, having obscurely the form of a man, with gleaming eyes, and bearing in his hand a blade. And I asked: "Who art thou?" But he answered: "I am a lascivious spirit, engendered of a giant man who died in the massacre in the time of the giants." I said to him: "Tell me what thou art employed upon earth, and where thou hast thy dwelling."

71. And he said: "My dwelling is in fruitful places, but my procedure is this. I seat myself beside the men who pass along among the tombs, and in untimely season I assume the form of the dead; and if I catch any one, I at once destroy him with my sword. But if I cannot destroy him, I cause him to be possessed with a demon, and to devour his own flesh, and the hair to fall off his chin." But I said to him: "Do thou then be in fear of the God of heaven and of earth, and tell me by what angel thou art frustrated." And he answered: "He destroys me who is to become Saviour, a man whose number, if any one shall write it on his forehead, he will defeat me, and in fear I shall quickly retreat. And, indeed, if any one write this sign on him, I shall be in fear." And I Solomon, on hearing this, and having glorified the Lord God, shut up this demon like the rest.

72. And I commanded another demon to come before me. And there came before my face thirty-six spirits, their heads shapeless like dogs, but in themselves they were human in form; with faces of asses, faces of oxen, and faces of birds. And I Solomon, on hearing and seeing them, wondered, and I asked them and said: "Who are you?" But they, of one accord with one voice, said1: "We are the thirty-six elements, the world-rulers of this darkness. (Eph. 6:12) But, O King Solomon, thou wilt not wrong us nor imprison us, nor lay command on us; but since the Lord God has given thee authority over every spirit, in the air, and on the earth, and under the earth, therefore do we also present ourselves before thee like the other spirits, from ram and bull, from both twin and crab, lion and virgin, scales and scorpion, archer, goat-horned, water-pourer, and fish."

73. Then I Solomon invoked the name of the Lord Sabaoth, and questioned each in turn as to what was its character. And I bade each one come forward and tell of its actions. Then the first one came forward, and said: "I am the first decan of the zodiacal circle, and I am called the Ram, and with me are these two." So I put to them the question: "Who are ye called?" The first said: "I, O Lord, am called Ruax, and I cause the heads of men to be idle, and I pillage their brows. But let me only hear the words, 'Michael, imprison Ruax,' and at once I retreat."

74. And the second said: "I am called Barsafael, and I cause those who are subject to my hour to feel the pain of migraine. If only I hear the words, 'Gabriel, imprison Barsafael,' at once I retreat.

75. The third said: "I am called Arôtosael. I do harm to eyes, and grievously injure them. Only let me hear the words, 'Uriel, imprison Aratosael', and at once I retreat."

76. The fifth said: "I am called Iudal, and I bring about a block in the ears and deafness of hearing. If I hear, 'Uruel Iudal,' I at once retreat."

77. The sixth said: "I am called Sphendonaêl. I cause tumors of the parotid gland, and inflammations of the tonsils, and tetanic recurvation. If I hear, 'Sabrael, imprison Sphendonaêl,' at once I retreat."

78. And the seventh said: "I am called Sphandôr, and I weaken the strength of the shoulders, and cause them to tremble; and I paralyze the nerves of the hands, and I break and bruise the bones of the neck. And I, I suck out the marrow. But if I hear the words, 'Araêl, imprison Sphandôr,' I at once retreat."

79. And the eighth said: "I am called Belbel. I distort the hearts and minds of men. If I hear the words, 'Araêl, imprison Belbel,' I at once retreat."

80. And the ninth said: "I am called Kurtaêl. I send colics in the bowels. I induce pains. If I hear the words, 'Iaôth, imprison Kurtaêl,' I at once retreat."

81. The tenth said: "I am called Metathiax. I cause the reins to ache. If I hear the words, 'Adônaêl, imprison Metathiax,' I at once retreat."

82. The eleventh said: "I am called Katanikotaêl. I create strife and wrongs in men's homes, and send on them hard tempers. If any one would be at peace in his home, let him write on seven leaves of laurel the name of the angel that frustrates me, along with these names: Iae, Ieô, sons of Sabaôth, in the name of the great God let him shut up Katanikotaêl. Then let him wash the laurel-leaves in water, and sprinkle his house with the water, from within to the outside. And at once I retreat."

83. The twelfth said: "I am called Saphathoraél, and I inspire partisanship in men, and delight in causing them to stumble. If any one will write on paper these names of angels, Iacô, Iealô, Iôelet, Sabaôth, Ithoth, Bae, and having folded it up; wear it round his neck or against his ear, I at once retreat and dissipate the drunken fit."

84. The thirteenth said: "I am called Bobêl, and I cause nervous illness by my assaults. If I hear the name of the great 'Adonaêl, imprison Bothothêl,' I at once retreat."

85. The fourteenth said: "I am called Kumeatêl, and I inflict shivering fits and torpor. If only I hear the words: 'Zôrôêl, imprison Kumentaêl,' I at once retreat."

86. The fifteenth said: "I am called Roêlêd. I cause cold and frost and pain in the stomach. Let me only hear the words: 'Iax, bide not, be not warmed, for Solomon is fairer than eleven fathers,' I at once retreat."

87. The sixteenth said: "I am called Atrax. I inflict upon men fevers, irremediable and harmful. If you would imprison me, chop up coriander and smear it on the lips, reciting the following charm: 'The fever which is from dirt. I exorcise thee by the throne of the most high God, retreat from dirt and retreat from the creature fashioned by God.' And at once I retreat."

88. The seventeenth said: "I am called Ieropaêl. On the stomach of men I sit, and cause convulsions in the bath and in the road; and wherever I be found, or find a man, I throw him down. But if any one will say to the afflicted into their ear these names, three times over, into the right ear: 'Iudarizê, Sabunê, Denôê,' I at once retreat."

89. The eighteenth said: "I am called Buldumêch. I separate wife from husband and bring about a grudge between them. If any one write down the names of thy sires, Solomon, on paper and place it in the ante-chamber of his house, I retreat thence. And the legend written shall be as follows: 'The God of Abram, and the God of Isaac, and the God of Jacob commands thee -- retire from this house in peace.' And I at once retire."

90. The nineteenth said: "I am called Naôth, and I take my seat on the knees of men. If any one write on paper: 'Phnunoboêol, depart Nathath, and touch thou not the neck,' I at once retreat."

91. The twentieth said: "I am called Marderô. I send on men incurable fever. If any one write on the leaf of a book: 'Sphênêr, Rafael, retire, drag me not about, flay me not,' and tie it round his neck, I at once retreat."

92. The twenty-first said: "I am called Alath, and I cause coughing and hard-breathing in children. If any one write on paper: 'Rorêx, do thou pursue Alath,' and fasten it round his neck, I at once retire."

93. The twenty-third said: "I am called Nefthada. I cause the reins to ache, and I bring about dysury. If any one write on a plate of tin the words: 'Iathôth, Uruêl, Nephthada,' and fasten it round the loins, I at once retreat."

94. The twenty-fourth said: "I am called Akton. I cause ribs and lumbar muscles to ache. If one engrave on copper material, taken from a ship which has missed its anchorage, this: 'Marmaraôth, Sabaôth, pursue Akton,' and fasten it round the loin, I at once retreat."

95. The twenty-fifth said: "I am called Anatreth, and I rend burnings and fevers into the entrails. But if I hear: 'Arara, Charara,' instantly do I retreat."

96. The twenty-sixth said: "I am called Enenuth. I steal away men's minds, and change their hearts, and make a man toothless. If one write: 'Allazoôl, pursue Enenuth,' and tie the paper round him, I at once retreat."

97. The twenty-seventh said: "I am called Phêth. I make men consumptive and cause hemorrhagia. If one exorcise me in wine, sweet-smelling and unmixed by the eleventh aeon, and say: 'I exorcise thee by the eleventh aeon to stop, I demand, Phêth (Axiôphêth),' then give it to the patient to drink I at once retreat."

98. The twenty-eighth said: "I am called Harpax, and I send sleeplessness on men. If one write 'Kokphnêdismos,' and bind it round the temples, I at once retire."

99. The twenty-ninth said: "I am called Anostêr. I engender uterine mania and pains in the bladder. If one powder into pure oil three seeds of laurel and smear it on, saying: 'I exorcise thee, Anostêr. Stop by Marmaraô,' at once I retreat."

100. The thirtieth said: "I am called Alleborith. If in eating fish one has swallowed a bone, then he must take a bone from the fish and cough, and at once I retreat."

101. The thirty-first said: "I am called Hephesimireth, and cause lingering disease. If you throw salt, rubbed in the hand, into oil and smear it on the patient, saying: 'Seraphim, Cherubim, help me!' I at once retire."

102. The thirty-second said: "I am called Ichthion. I paralyze muscles and contuse them. If I hear 'Adonaêth, help!' I at once retire."

103. The thirty-third said: "I am called Agchoniôn. I lie among swaddling-clothes and in the precipice. And if any one write on fig-leaves 'Lycurgos,' taking away one letter at a time, and write it, reversing the letters, I retire at once. 'Lycurgos, Ycurgos, Kurgos, Yrgos, Gos, Os.'"

104. The thirty-fourth said: "I am called Autothith. I cause grudges and fighting. Therefore I am frustrated by Alpha and Omega, if written down."

105. The thirty-fifth said: "I am called Phthenoth. I cast evil eyes on every man. Therefore, the drawing of the eye causes me much suffering, it frustrates me."

106. The thirty-sixth said: "I am called Bianakith. I have a grudge against the body. I lay waste to houses, I cause flesh to decay and all else that is similar. If a man write on the front-door of his house: 'Mêltô, Ardu, Anaath,' I flee from that place."

107. And I Solomon, when I heard this, glorified the God of heaven and earth. And I commanded them to fetch water in the Temple of God. And I furthermore prayed to the Lord God to cause the demons without, that hamper humanity, to be bound and made to approach the Temple of God. Some of these demons I condemned to do the heavy work of the construction of the Temple of God. Others I shut up in prisons. Others I ordered to wrestle with fire in the making of gold and silver, sitting down by lead and spoon. And to make ready places for the other demons in which they should be confined.

108. And I Solomon had much quiet in all the earth, and spent my life in profound peace, honored by all men and by all under heaven. And I built the entire Temple of the Lord God. And my kingdom was prosperous, and my army was with me. And for the rest, the city of Jerusalem had repose, rejoicing and delighted. And all the kings of the earth came to me from the ends of the earth to behold the Temple which I built unto the Lord God. And having heard of the wisdom given to me, they paid homage to me in the Temple, bringing gold and silver and precious stones, many and divers, and bronze, and iron, and lead, and cedar logs. And woods that decay not they brought me, for the equipment of the Temple of God.

109. And among them also the queen of the South, being a witch, came in great concern and bowed low before me to the earth. And having heard my wisdom, she glorified the God of Israel, and she made formal trial of all my wisdom, of all disciplines in which I instructed her, according to the wisdom imparted to me. And all the sons of Israel glorified God.

110. And behold, in those days one of the workmen, of ripe old age, threw himself down before me, and said: "King Solomon, pity me, because I am old." So I bade him stand up, and said: "Tell me, old man, all you will." And he answered: "I beseech you king, I have an only-born son, and he insults and beats me openly, and plucks out the hair of my head, and threatens me with a painful death. Therefore I beseech you avenge me."

111. And I Solomon, on hearing this, felt compunction as I looked at his old age; and I bade the child be brought to me. And when he was brought I questioned him whether it were true. And the youth said: "I was not so filled with madness as to strike my father with my hand. Be kind to me, O king. For I have not dared to commit such impiety, poor wretch that I am." But I Solomon on hearing this from the youth, exhorted the old man to reflect on the matter, and accept his son's apology. However, he would not, but said he would rather let him die. And as the old man would not yield, I was about to pronounce sentence on the youth, when I saw Ornias the demon laughing. I was very angry at the demon's laughing in my presence; and I ordered my men to remove the other parties, and bring forward

Ornias before my tribunal. And when he was brought before me, I said to him: "Accursed one, why didst thou look at me and laugh?" And the demon answered: "Prithee, king, it was not because of thee I laughed, but because of this ill-starred old man and the wretched youth, his son. For after three days his son will die untimely; and lo, the old man desires to foully make away with him."

112. But I Solomon, having heard this, said to the demon: "Is that true that thou speakest?" And he answered: "It is true; O king." And I, on hearing that, bade them remove the demon, and that they should again bring before me the old man with his son. I bade them make friends with one another again, and I supplied them with food. And then I told the old man after three days to bring his son again to me here; "and," said I, "I will attend to him." And they saluted me, and went their way.

113. And when they were gone I ordered Ornias to be brought forward, and said to him: "Tell me how you know this!" and he answered: "We demons ascend into the firmament of heaven, and fly about among the stars. And we hear the sentences which go forth upon the souls of men, and forthwith we come, and whether by force of influence, or by fire, or by sword, or by some accident, we veil our act of destruction; and if a man does not die by some untimely disaster or by violence, then we demons transform ourselves in such a way as to appear to men and be worshipped in our human nature."

114. I therefore, having heard this, glorified the Lord God, and again I questioned the demon, saying: "Tell me how ye can ascend into heaven, being demons, and amidst the stars and holy angels intermingle." And he answered: "Just as things are fulfilled in heaven, so also on earth they are fulfilled the types of all of them. For there are principalities, authorities, world-rulers, and we demons fly about in the air; and we hear the voices of the heavenly beings, and survey all the powers. And as having no ground (basis) on which to alight and rest, we lose strength and fall off like leaves from trees. And men seeing us imagine that the stars are falling from heaven. But it is not really so, O king; but we fall because of our weakness, and because we have nowhere anything to lay hold of; and so we fall down like lightnings in the depth of night and suddenly. And we set cities in flames and fire the fields. For the stars have firm foundations in the heavens like the sun and the moon."

115. And I Solomon, having heard this, ordered the demon to be guarded for five days. And after the five days I recalled the old man, and was about to question him. But he came to me in grief and with black face. And I said to him: "Tell me, old man, where is thy son? And what means this garb?" And he answered: "Lo, I am become childless and sit by my son's grave in despair. For it is already two

days that he is dead." But I Solomon, on hearing that, and knowing that the demon Ornias had told me the truth, glorified the God of Israel.

116. And the queen of the South saw all this, and marvelled by glorifying the God of Israel; and she beheld the Temple of the Lord being built. And she gave a shekel of gold and one hundred myriads of silver and choice bronze, and she went into the Temple. And she beheld the altar of incense and the brazen supports of this altar, and the gems of the lamps flashing forth of different colors, and of the lamp-stand of stone, and of emerald, and hyacinth, and sapphire; and she beheld the vessels of gold, and silver, and bronze, and wood, and the folds of skins dyed red with madder. And she saw the bases of the pillars of the Temple of the Lord. All were of one gold (Manuscript too badly damaged to read) apart from the demons whom I condemned to labor thereon. And there was peace in the circle of my kingdom and over all the earth.

117. And it came to pass, which I was in my kingdom, the King of the Arabians, Adares, sent me a letter, and the writing of the letter was written as follows:

"To King Solomon, all hail! Lo, we have heard, and it hath been heard unto all the ends of the earth, concerning the wisdom entrusted in thee, and that thou art a man merciful from the Lord. And understanding hath been granted thee over all the spirits of the air, and on earth, and under the earth. Now, forasmuch as there is present in the land of Arabia a spirit of the following kind: at early dawn there begins to blow a certain wind until the third hour. And its blast is harsh and terrible, and it slays man and beast. And no spirit can live upon earth against this demon. I pray thee then, forasmuch as the spirit is a wind, contrive something according to the wisdom given in thee by the Lord thy God, and deign to send a man able to capture it. And behold, King Solomon, I and my people and all my land will serve thee unto death. And all Arabia shall be at peace with thee, if thou wilt perform this act of righteousness for us. Wherefore we pray thee, condemn not our humble prayer, and suffer not to be utterly brought to naught the eparchy subordinated to thy authority. Because we are suppliants, both I and my people and all my land. Farewell to my Lord. All health!"

118. And I Solomon read this epistle; and I folded it up and gave it to my people, and said to them: "After seven days shalt thou remind me of this epistle. And Jerusalem was built, and the Temple was being completed. And there was a stone, the end stone of the corner lying there, great, chosen out, one which I desired lay

in the head of the corner of the completion of the Temple. And all the workmen, and all the demons helping them came to the same place to bring up the stone and lay it on the pinnacle of the holy Temple, and were not strong enough to stir it, and lay it upon the corner allotted to it. For that stone was exceedingly great and useful for the corner of the Temple."

119. And after seven days, being reminded of the epistle of Adares, King of Arabia, I called my servant and said to him: "Order thy camel and take for thyself a leather flask, and take also this seal. And go away into Arabia to the place in which the evil spirit blows; and there take the flask, and the signet-ring in front of the mouth of the flask, and hold them together towards the blast of the spirit. And when the flask is blown out, thou wilt understand that the demon is in it. Then hastily tie up the mouth of the flask, and seal it securely with the seal-ring, and lay it carefully on the camel and bring it me hither. And if on the way it offer thee gold or silver or treasure in return for letting it go, see that thou be not persuaded. But arrange without using oath to release it. And then if it point out to the places where are gold or silver, mark the places and seal them with this seal. And bring the demon to me. And now depart, and fare thee well."

120. Then the youth did as was bidden him. And he ordered his camel, and laid on it a flask, and set off into Arabia. And the men of that region would not believe that he would be able to catch the evil spirit. And when it was dawn, the servant stood before the spirit's blast, and laid the flask on the ground, and the finger-ring on the mouth of the flask. And the demon blew through the middle of the finger-ring into the mouth of the flask, and going in blew out the flask. But the man promptly stood up to it and drew tight with his hand the mouth of the flask, in the name of the Lord God of Sabaôth. And the demon remained within the flask. And after that the youth remained in that land three days to make trial. And the spirit no longer blew against that city. And all the Arabs knew that he had safely shut in the spirit.

121. Then the youth fastened the flask on the camel, and the Arabs sent him forth on his way with much honor and precious gifts, praising and magnifying the God of Israel. But the youth brought in the bag and laid it in the middle of the Temple. And on the next day, I King Solomon, went into the Temple of God and sat in deep distress about the stone of the end of the corner. And when I entered the Temple, the flask stood up and walked around some seven steps and then fell on its mouth and paid homage to me. And I marvelled that even along with the bottle the demon still had power and could walk about; and I commanded it to stand up. And the flask stood up, and stood on its feet all blown out. And I questioned him, saying: "Tell me, who art thou?" And the spirit within said: "I am the demon called Ephippas, that is in Arabia." And I said to him: "Is this thy

name?" And he answered: "Yes; wheresoever I will, I alight and set fire and do to death."

122. And I said to him: "By what angel art thou frustrated?" And he answered: "By the only-ruling God, that hath authority over me even to be heard. He that is to be born of a virgin and crucified by the Jews on a cross. Whom the angels and archangels worship. He doth frustrate me, and enfeeble me of my great strength, which has been given me by my father Satan." And I said to him: "What canst thou do?" And he answered: "I am able to remove mountains, to overthrow the oaths of kings. I wither trees and make their leaves fall off." And I said to him: "Canst thou raise this stone, and lay it for the beginning of this corner which exists in the fair plan of the Temple?" And he said: "Not only raise this, O king; but also, with the help of the demon who presides over the Red Sea, I will bring up the pillar of air, and will stand it where thou wilt in Jerusalem."

123. Saying this, I laid stress on him, and the flask became as if depleted of air. And I placed it under the stone, and the spirit girded himself up, and lifted it up top of the flask. And the flask went up the steps, carrying the stone, and laid it down at the end of the entrance of the Temple. And I Solomon, beholding the stone raised aloft and placed on a foundation, said: "Truly the Scripture is fulfilled, which says: 'The stone which the builders rejected on trial, that same is become the head of the corner.' For this it is not mine to grant, but God's, that the demon should be strong enough to lift up so great a stone and deposit it in the place I wished."

124. And Ephippas led the demon of the Red Sea with the column. And they both took the column and raised it aloft from the earth. And I outwitted these two spirits, so that they could not shake the entire earth in a moment of time. And then I sealed round with my signet ring on this side and that, and said: "Watch!" And the spirits have remained upholding it until this day, for proof of the wisdom entrusted unto me. And there the pillar was hanging of enormous size, in mid air, supported by the winds. And thus the spirits appeared underneath, like air, supporting it. And if one looks fixedly, the pillar is a little oblique, being supported by the spirits; and it is so to day.

125. And I Solomon questioned the other spirit which came up with the pillar from the depth of the Red Sea. And I said to him: "Who art thou, and what calls thee? And what is thy business? For I hear many things about thee." And the demon answered: "I, O King Solomon, am called Abezithibod. I am a descendant of the archangel. Once as I sat in the first heaven, of which the name is Ameleouth -- I then am a fierce spirit and winged, and with a single wing, plotting against every spirit under heaven. I was present when Moses went in before Pharaoh, king of Egypt, and I hardened his heart. I am he whom Iannes

and Iambres invoked homing with Moses in Egypt. I am he who fought against Moses with wonders with signs."

126. I said therefore to him: "How wast thou found in the Red Sea?" And he answered: "In the exodus of the sons of Israel I hardened the heart of Pharaoh. And I excited his heart and that of his ministers. And I caused them to pursue after the children of Israel. And Pharaoh followed with me and all the Egyptians. Then I was present there, and we followed together. And we all came up upon the Red Sea. And it came to pass when the children of Israel had crossed over, the water returned and crushed all the host of the Egyptians and all their might. And I remained in the sea, being kept under this pillar. But when Ephippas came, being sent by thee, shut up in the vessel of a flask, he fetched me up to thee."

127. I, therefore, Solomon, having heard this, glorified God and adjured the demons not to disobey me, but to remain supporting the pillar. And they both swore an oath, saying: "As the Lord thy God liveth, we will not let go this pillar until the world's end. But on whatever day this stone fall, then shall be the beginning of the end of the world."

128. And I Solomon glorified God, and adorned the Temple of the Lord with all fair-seeming. And I was glad in spirit in my kingdom, and there was peace in my days. And I took wives of my own from every land, who were numberless. And I marched against the Jebusaeans, and there I saw a Jebusaean, daughter of a man: and fell violently in love with her, and desired to take her to wife along with my other wives. And I said to their priests: "Give me the Sonmanites (i.e. Shunammite) to wife." (Song of Solomon 6:13) But the priests of Moloch said to me: "If thou lovest this maiden, go in and worship our gods, the great god Raphan and the god called Moloch." I therefore was in fear of the glory of God, and did not follow to worship. And I said to them: "I will not worship a demon. What is this proposal, that ye compel me to do so much?" But they said: "It is to be done according to our fathers."

129. And when I answered that I would on no account worship demons, they told the maiden not to sleep with me until I complied and sacrificed to their gods. I then was moved, but crafty Eros brought and laid by her for me five grasshoppers, saying: "Take these grasshoppers, and crush them together in the name of the god Moloch; and then will I sleep with you." And this I did. And at once the Spirit of God departed from me, and I became weak as well as foolish in my words. And after that I was obliged by her to build a temple of idols to Baal, and to Rapha, and to Moloch, and to the other demons.

130. I then, wretch that I am, followed her advice, and the glory of God departed from me; and my spirit was darkened, and I became the sport of idols and demons. Wherefore I wrote out this Testament, that ye who get possession of it may pity, and attend to the last things, and not to the first. So that ye may find grace for ever and ever. Amen.

CLOSING STATEMENTS / ANALYSIS

The Testament of Solomon is important for several reasons. Primarily because it deals with the spirits of the fallen giants. You see, since the giants were born of the fallen angels through women, their spirits were different to that of men. They, unlike mankind, doesn't go to the grave in rest awaiting a resurrection and judgment. They can roam the earth as they wish or until they are imprisoned by God. In this testament did Solomon encounter the spirits of the giants which further amplifies the existence of their fallen nature. That, even after the death of the giants, they still lived through other bodies and forms.

With a clear hatred of mankind, as was demonstrated during their fleshly lives, so too do they continue carrying out their vengeance upon mankind after their fleshly bodies expired. Not being confined to flesh, but able to inhabit flesh, and any form of matter - became their existence after their deaths. Disembodied spirits they would become. As you've read, Solomon summoned them to come before him. After Solomon's death, despite his very noble attempt to seal up the vessels containing the demons (spirits of the giants), did a group of nine knights find them. The Knights of the Templar, or Knights of the Temple Mount. They named themselves this because they excavated Solomon's temple for nearly a decade before they finally found what they were looking for: Solomon's ring, and the vessels he had sealed up the demons in.

After the knights had returned to Europe with their finds did the Catholic church honor them and give them riches beyond belief. They invented the modern day checking system and began bank rolling anyone they could. They black mailed several lords with threats of demonic activity, and even sometimes delivered on their promises. This of course didn't go unnoticed and eventually the Catholic church had them burned at the stake for consorting with the devil. Many of them died on Friday the 13th but not all of them were slaughtered. The ones who escaped would later form Freemasonry and the Illuminati. And so the book goes, you may be through with the past but the past isn't through with you.

Printed in Great Britain
by Amazon